THE EMPOWERED WOMAN SERIES

A Journey to Emotional Freedom, Balance, and Lasting Inner Peace

---

EVE MEADOWS

Contents

Women Breaking Free

Women Embracing Peace

Women Breaking Free

CONQUER CONTROL ISSUES, OVERCOME PERFECTIONISM, REDUCE ANXIETY, ACHIEVE WORK-LIFE BALANCE, AND FIND INNER PEACE FOR EMOTIONAL WELL-BEING

Introduction

I remember the moment like it was yesterday. I was standing in my kitchen, frantically organizing the cabinets while simultaneously planning the week's meals in my head. The kids were squabbling in the background, my phone buzzing with work emails, and my partner asked me where his clean socks were. I snapped. The pressure of managing every detail, of controlling every outcome, was overwhelming, and I broke down in tears. Sound familiar?

You might be reading this and nodding your head. Maybe you've had moments of feeling like you're holding the world together with duct tape and sheer willpower. If you're a woman juggling multiple roles —professional, partner, mother, friend—you know all too well the stress of trying to control everything. This constant need to manage all aspects of life often leads to anxiety, strained relationships, and a sense of burnout that's hard to shake.

So, what does it mean to be a control freak? It's not a term I use lightly. Being a control freak involves a persistent need to ensure everything around you goes according to plan. It's micromanaging at work because you believe that no one else can do the job as well as you can. It's organizing every family outing down to the minute, fearing that any deviation will lead to chaos. It's the anxiety that bubbles up when things don't go as expected and the frustration that comes from trying to manage outcomes beyond your control.

Control issues are more widespread than you might think. According to various studies, many women feel overwhelmed by the need to control their environments. This behavior is often driven by societal pressures to be perfect in every role we play. The impact on mental health is significant, leading to increased stress, anxiety, and depression. Relationships also suffer, as the need for control can create tension and conflict with loved ones.

I've been there. I've struggled with control issues for years. My wake-up call came when I realized my need to control everything drove a wedge between me and the people I cared about most. I was constantly stressed, racing with to-do lists and contingency plans. I knew something had to change. My journey towards letting go of control wasn't easy, but it was transformative. I learned to embrace uncertainty, to trust others, and to find peace in the present moment. This book reflects that journey and the lessons I've learned.

My vision for this book is simple yet powerful: to empower you to let go of control and embrace a life of balance, peace, and fulfillment. We'll explore practical tools, self-reflection exercises, and holistic strategies to help you manage anxiety, improve relationships, and thrive personally and professionally. This isn't about perfection; it's about progress and growth.

The book is structured to guide you through this transformative process step by step. We'll start by understanding the roots of control issues and how they manifest in your daily life. Then, we'll dive into strategies for enhancing self-awareness and developing healthier thought patterns. You'll find practical advice on managing stress, setting boundaries, and nurturing your emotional well-being. Each chapter ends with reflection exercises to help you apply your learning.

Who is this book for? It's for women like you who are seeking personal growth and balance. It's for those in relationships wanting to improve dynamics and individuals struggling with anxiety and control issues. It's for professional women, parents, and anyone navigating the complex web of societal and cultural expectations. If you're ready to break free from the constraints of control and perfectionism, this book is for you.

I want you to know that this journey won't be perfect, and that's okay. The tone of this book is supportive, empathetic, and informal. I'm here with you every step of the way, offering guidance and encouragement. The advice is easy to follow, with actionable steps and relatable examples to help you make meaningful changes in your life.

Self-awareness is the key to overcoming control issues. By understanding the root causes of your behaviors, you can begin to make conscious choices that lead to healthier, more fulfilling relationships and a more balanced life. This book will guide you through that process, helping you to see yourself and your actions more clearly.

I promise you that transformation is possible. Following this book's guidance, you'll learn to manage anxiety, improve relationships, and thrive personally and professionally. You deserve a life that isn't dictated by the need to control everything. You deserve peace, balance, and fulfillment. Let's take this journey together.

Welcome to a new chapter in your life.

ONE

Understanding Control Behaviors

I once had a friend who would meticulously plan every detail of our weekend getaways. From the exact route we'd take to the type of snacks we'd have, she left no stone unturned. While her organization skills were impressive, they often left little room for spontaneity or relaxation. While seemingly harmless, this need to control every aspect of our trips was a manifestation of deeper control issues. You're not alone if you've ever been in a similar situation. Many of us struggle with the need to control our environments and the people in them, often without even realizing it.

Recognizing the Signs of Control

Control behaviors can be overt and subtle, but they all share a common thread: the need to manage and influence outcomes. Micromanaging tasks are a classic example. You might feel compelled to oversee every detail of a project at work, believing that no one else can execute it to your standards. Insisting on specific ways of doing things, whether it's the laundry or how the dishwasher is loaded, also falls under this umbrella. You may find it difficult to delegate responsibilities, worrying that others won't meet your expectations. This leads to excessive checking and reassurances, constantly verifying that tasks are done "correctly."

Common behaviors signaling a tendency towards control include interrupting others to assert your opinions and becoming anxious when plans change. You might also find yourself constantly correcting others, whether it's your partner's way of folding clothes or your colleague's approach to a task. While seemingly minor, these actions can indicate a deeper issue with control.

Consider these relatable scenarios: A mother meticulously correcting her child's homework, not allowing any room for mistakes, or a manager redoing employee tasks, believing her way is the only right way. These situations create stress and stifle creativity and growth in those around you.

The emotional drivers behind control behaviors are often rooted in fear and anxiety. Fear of failure can make you feel that controlling every aspect of your life will prevent mistakes. Anxiety about the unknown can lead you to over-plan and over-manage, seeking comfort in predictability.

Understanding these signs and emotional drivers is the first step in recognizing and addressing control behaviors. By becoming aware of these tendencies, you can make conscious choices to let go of control, fostering a more balanced and fulfilling life.

The Psychology Behind Control

Understanding the psychology behind control behaviors can be enlightening. Cognitive-behavioral theories offer insights into how our thoughts influence our actions. Cognitive distortions, or faulty thinking patterns, can lead us to believe control is the only way to prevent failure. For instance, black-and-white thinking can make us see situations as perfect or disastrous, pushing us to control every detail to avoid perceived catastrophes. Similarly, overgeneralization can lead us to apply one negative experience to all future situations, reinforcing the need for control.

Attachment theory also plays a significant role in understanding control behaviors. Insecure attachment styles, often developed in childhood, can lead to a heightened need for control in adulthood. If you experienced overprotective parenting, you might have learned that the world is dangerous and controlling every aspect of your environment is the only way to navigate it. Childhood trauma, such as neglect or abuse, can further exacerbate these feelings, making you feel that control is necessary for safety and stability.

Personality traits are another critical factor. Perfectionism, characterized by setting unrealistically high standards, is often linked to control behaviors. Perfectionists may fear making mistakes and feel compelled to control every detail to ensure everything meets their exacting standards. High conscientiousness, the desire for order, structure, and dependability, can also contribute to control behaviors. While these traits can be strengths, they can lead to stress and anxiety when taken to extremes.

Societal and cultural factors cannot be ignored. Societal pressure to succeed, particularly for women, can drive control behaviors. We are often expected to excel in multiple roles—career, family, social life— leading us to believe that control is the only way to meet these expectations. Cultural norms around gender roles also play a part. Traditional expectations that women should manage the household, care for children, and support partners can create an overwhelming sense of responsibility, further fueling the need for control.

Understanding these psychological underpinnings helps us see that control behaviors are not merely quirks but deeply rooted responses to various influences. Recognizing the impact of cognitive distortions, attachment styles, personality traits, and societal pressures allows us to approach the issue with empathy and self-awareness. By exploring these factors, we can unravel the complex web that drives our need for control and take the first steps toward a more balanced and fulfilling life.

How Control Manifests in Daily Life

Control behaviors often seep into the fabric of our daily routines, shaping how we organize and manage our lives. Planning and organizing routines can feel like a lifeline in the chaotic responsibilities swirl. You might find comfort in mapping out every minute of your day, from when you wake up to when you go to bed. This meticulous planning can provide a sense of control and predictability, but it can also become a rigid framework that leaves little room for spontaneity or flexibility. When every aspect of your day is scheduled to the last second, any unexpected event can throw you into a tailspin of anxiety and frustration.

Controlling household chores is another common manifestation. You may need to oversee every task, ensuring everything is done "your way." This could mean dictating how the laundry is folded, how the dishwasher is loaded, or even how the groceries are organized in the pantry. While it's natural to have preferences, insisting on specific ways of doing things can create a tense atmosphere at home. This behavior can also lead to resentment from family members who feel micromanaged and undervalued, straining relationships and creating unnecessary stress.

In professional settings, control behaviors can be both a blessing and a curse. Micromanaging team projects stems from a desire to ensure high-quality outcomes, but it can stifle creativity and autonomy among team members. When you're constantly checking in on every detail, it sends a message that you don't trust others to do their jobs effectively. This can lead to a toxic work environment where colleagues feel demotivated and disengaged. Reluctance to delegate tasks is another hallmark of control in the workplace. By taking on too much yourself, you not only overwhelm your workload but also deny others the opportunity to grow and contribute.

Control behaviors also permeate personal relationships, often in subtle ways. You might find yourself dictating social plans, insisting on specific activities, venues, or schedules. This can make your friends or partner feel like their preferences don't matter, leading to a sense of imbalance in the relationship. Monitoring your partner's actions, whether it's through constant check-ins or subtle surveillance, can erode trust and intimacy. This behavior often stems from a fear of unpredictability or loss, but it can push your partner away and create emotional distance.

Parenting is another area where control can manifest strongly. Over-scheduling your children's activities, from extracurriculars to playdates, might seem like a way to ensure their success and well-being. However, it can also rob them of the freedom to explore, make mistakes, and develop their interests. Setting rigid rules and expectations can create a high-pressure environment that stifles their creativity and independence. Children may feel like they're constantly under scrutiny, leading to anxiety and a fear of failure.

Understanding how control behaviors permeate daily life is crucial for recognizing their impact. By becoming aware of these tendencies, you can make conscious choices to let go of control, fostering a more balanced and fulfilling life.

The Impact of Control on Mental Health

The link between control behaviors and anxiety is profound. When you constantly strive to control every aspect of your life, it creates a state of hypervigilance. Your mind is always on high alert, scanning for potential problems and planning for every possible outcome. This constant worry can be exhausting. You might find yourself lying awake at night, unable to shut off your thoughts, leading to chronic sleep issues. Physical symptoms often accompany this mental strain —headaches, fatigue, and even digestive problems become your unwelcome companions. The body and mind are in a perpetual state of stress, and it's a heavy burden to carry.

Control behaviors also take a toll on self-esteem. When you set impossibly high standards, and things inevitably fall short, feelings of inadequacy creep in. You might start to believe that you're not good enough, that your worth is somehow tied to your ability to manage everything perfectly. This can lead to imposter syndrome, where you feel like a fraud despite your accomplishments. You might constantly fear being exposed as incapable or unworthy, leading to even more controlled behaviors to mask these insecurities. The cycle is vicious and self-perpetuating, eroding your sense of self-worth bit by bit.

The broader consequences on overall well-being are equally concerning. The relentless pursuit of control puts you at a heightened risk for burnout. You're constantly juggling, always one step away from dropping everything. This chronic stress can sap your energy, leaving you exhausted and emotionally drained. Over time, this can lead to more severe mental health issues such as depression. The joy and spontaneity of life fade away, replaced by a rigid, colorless existence where every moment is planned and every outcome is scrutinized.

Let's talk about real-life impact. Sarah, a dedicated professional in her mid-thirties, was the epitome of success on the outside. She managed her team with an iron grip, ensuring every project met her exacting standards. However, the constant stress took its toll. She began experiencing severe headaches and fatigue, struggling to find motivation. Her relationships with her colleagues became strained as her micromanaging left them feeling undervalued. Eventually, Sarah reached a breaking point, realizing her need for control was unsustainable. Seeking help, she learned to delegate and trust her team, slowly rebuilding her work-life balance and mental health.

Consider Nina, a mother who orchestrated every detail of her family's life. From school projects to family vacations, everything had to be perfect. She believed that by controlling these aspects, she was ensuring the best for her children. However, the constant pressure led to severe anxiety and frequent panic attacks. Nina felt like a failure whenever things didn't go as planned, and her self-esteem plummeted. After a particularly intense episode, she decided to seek therapy. Through counseling, she learned to let go of her need for control, embracing a more flexible approach to parenting. Her mental health improved, and her relationships with her children flourished.

Understanding the impact of control on your mental health is crucial. Recognizing these patterns and their consequences can be the first step toward change. By addressing the root causes and learning to let go, you can reclaim your well-being and live a more balanced, fulfilling life.

How Control Affects Relationships

Control behaviors can wreak havoc on romantic relationships, creating a web of tension and conflict that's hard to untangle. Imagine planning a romantic dinner, only to find yourself micromanaging every detail—from the menu to the seating arrangement—because you believe it's the only way to ensure a perfect evening. This need to control your partner's choices can lead to resentment, even in small matters. Over time, your partner may feel stifled, as though their preferences and autonomy don't matter.

This lack of trust and open communication can breed bitterness and emotional distance, making it difficult for intimacy and genuine connection to flourish.

Friendships aren't immune to the grasp of control either. You might dominate conversations, always steering the topic back to your interests or concerns. This behavior can leave your friends feeling unheard and undervalued, slowly eroding the foundation of your relationship. Dictating group activities, insisting on specific plans, and not allowing others to contribute can further strain these bonds. Friends may start to feel that their opinions and desires are secondary, which can lead to frustration and disengagement. Over time, this can result in a social circle that feels more like a chore than a source of support and joy.

Family dynamics can also suffer under the weight of control behaviors. For instance, constantly correcting your children or setting overly rigid rules can create a high-pressure environment. This strains your relationship with them and can exacerbate sibling rivalry. One child might feel favored or more trusted than the other, leading to jealousy and conflict. In a broader sense, family members might start to feel like they're walking on eggshells, always worried about meeting your high standards. This can create an emotionally charged atmosphere where genuine communication and support are hard to maintain.

Improving these relationships requires consciously letting go of control and fostering mutual respect and trust. One effective strategy is practicing active listening. This means genuinely hearing what the other person is saying without planning your rebuttal or steering the conversation. It's about validating their feelings and showing empathy. Building mutual trust is another crucial element. Trust is a two-way street; it requires both giving and receiving. Show your partner, friends, and family that you trust them by allowing them to make decisions and respecting their choices.

Consider small steps, like letting your partner choose the restaurant for your next date night or allowing your children to decide on a weekend activity. These actions might seem minor, but they send a powerful message of trust and respect. Gradually, these efforts can help mend the strained threads of your relationships, creating a more balanced and fulfilling dynamic.

Self-Assessment: Are You a Control Freak?

One of the most enlightening steps in overcoming control issues is self-awareness. I've designed a self-assessment tool to help you gauge where you stand. This questionnaire will guide you through various aspects of your daily routines, habits, and responses to change.

Let's start with a few questions about your everyday habits:

1. How often do you redo tasks because they weren't done your way?
2. Do you feel anxious when someone else is handling something you usually manage?
3. How do you react when plans change unexpectedly?
4. Are you comfortable delegating tasks to others, or do you prefer to do everything yourself to ensure it's done correctly?

Next, let's consider some scenarios to understand your responses to change:

1. Imagine you've planned a weekend getaway, but sudden weather changes disrupt your plans. How do you handle the situation?
2. Your partner decides to cook dinner but doesn't follow the recipe to the letter. What's your immediate reaction?

3. At work, a project deadline is moved up unexpectedly. What's your first course of action?

Now, let's talk about scoring and interpretation. Each question is designed to reflect a spectrum of control behaviors. You'll score each response on a scale from 1 (rarely) to 5 (always).

Here's a simple scoring rubric:

- 0-15: You exhibit minimal control behaviors.
- 16-30: You have moderate control tendencies.
- 31-45: Your control behaviors are significant and may impact your life and relationships.

Interpreting your score is crucial. A lower score indicates that control isn't a significant issue for you, but staying mindful is worthwhile. A moderate score suggests that while you manage well most of the time, certain triggers can bring out control behaviors. A high score means control is a significant part of your life, and addressing it could lead to healthier relationships and improved well-being.

For personalized feedback, those with high scores will benefit from tailored advice. Focus on small steps to delegate tasks and embrace flexibility. For those with moderate scores, work on identifying specific triggers and developing coping mechanisms. Lower scores should maintain their current balance while remaining vigilant for emerging control behaviors.

Follow-up actions can vary based on your score. Seeking professional help, such as therapy, can benefit high scores. Therapists can provide structured support and techniques tailored to your needs. Engaging in self-help activities is another effective route. Consider mindfulness practices, journaling, or joining support groups focused on reducing control behaviors.

Self-awareness is the cornerstone of change. Understanding your control tendencies allows you to take actionable steps toward a more balanced and fulfilling life. This assessment is just the beginning. Embrace its insights and use them as a foundation for growth and transformation.

TWO

Practical Tools for Immediate Change

Imagine waking up in the morning without the heavy weight of anxiety pressing down on your chest. The day's tasks are still there but feel like a manageable mountain. Instead, you feel a sense of calm and control—not the controlling kind, but the kind that comes from within. This sense of peace might seem elusive, but it's within reach, and mindfulness is a powerful tool to help you get there.

Mindfulness Techniques to Calm the Mind

Mindfulness is about being present in the moment without judgment. It's a simple concept but incredibly powerful in reducing controlling behaviors. At its core, mindfulness means paying attention to what you're doing as you're doing it. When you're mindful, you're fully engaged in the present, which leaves less room for anxious thoughts about the past or future.

The benefits of mindfulness for mental health are well-documented. Studies have shown that mindfulness can reduce symptoms of anxiety and depression, improve concentration, and increase emotional regulation. Practicing mindfulness can break the cycle of overthinking and over-controlling, leading to a more balanced and fulfilling life.

Let's start with some simple mindfulness exercises. One effective technique is the body scan meditation. Find a quiet space where you won't be disturbed. Sit or lie comfortably, close your eyes, and take a few deep breaths. Starting from the top of your head, slowly move your attention down through your body, noticing any sensations without trying to change them. If your mind wanders, gently bring it back to the present moment. This exercise helps you become more aware of your physical sensations, reducing the urge to control your environment.

Another accessible practice is mindful walking. As you walk, focus on the sensation of your feet touching the ground, the movement of your legs, and the rhythm of your breath. Notice your surroundings —the colors, the sounds, the smells—without getting lost in thought. This simple act of walking with awareness can ground you in the present moment and alleviate anxiety.

Incorporating mindfulness into daily routines can make a significant difference. Mindful eating is a great place to start. Instead of rushing through meals, take the time to savor each bite. Notice the flavors, textures, and aromas of your food. Eating mindfully enhances your dining experience and helps you tune into your body's hunger and fullness cues, promoting healthier eating habits.

Mindfulness can also be integrated into household chores. For example, while washing dishes, focus on the sensation of the water, the movement of your hands, and the sound of the clinking dishes. By turning mundane tasks into opportunities for mindfulness, you can transform daily routines into moments of calm and clarity.

Consider the story of Emily, a high-powered executive who used mindfulness to regain control over her life. She started practicing mindfulness during her lunch breaks, taking just ten minutes to focus on her breath and clear her mind. This simple change helped her manage work stress and improved her productivity. She incorporated mindfulness into family time at home, leading to more meaningful connections with her children.

Or take Lisa, a mother of two, who was constantly overwhelmed by her kids' schedules and household responsibilities. She began practicing mindfulness with her children, turning bedtime into a calming ritual of deep breathing and gratitude. This not only reduced her anxiety but also created a peaceful bedtime routine for her kids.

Deep-Breathing Exercises for Instant Stress Relief

Ever notice how a few deep breaths can instantly calm you down? There's science behind it. Deep breathing activates the parasympathetic nervous system, the body's natural way of hitting the "calm down" button. This system slows your heart rate and reduces cortisol—the stress hormone that makes you feel like the sky is falling. When cortisol levels drop, your body and mind relax, making it easier to let go of the need to control every little thing.

Let's start with the box breathing method. This exercise is simple but effective. Find a comfortable seat and close your eyes. Inhale deeply through your nose for a count of four. Hold your breath for another count of four. Exhale slowly through your mouth for four, then hold your breath again for four. Repeat this cycle several times. This method calms your mind and helps you regain focus, making it easier to navigate stressful situations without feeling the need to control them.

Another great technique is the 4-7-8 breathing method. This exercise is beneficial for reducing anxiety and promoting relaxation. Here's how you do it: Sit or lie down comfortably. Close your eyes and inhale quietly through your nose for a count of four. Hold your breath for a count of seven. Then, exhale completely through your mouth, making a whoosh sound for a count of eight. Repeat this cycle three to four times. The 4-7-8 method works by regulating your breath, which helps calm the nervous system, making it easier to let go of control and embrace the present moment.

Incorporating these breathing exercises into your daily routine can make a significant difference. Start your day with a morning breathing ritual. Before getting out of bed, practice the box breathing or 4-7-8 method for a few minutes. This sets a calm tone for the day and prepares you to easily handle whatever comes your way. During work, take short breathing breaks. Set a reminder on your phone or computer to pause for a quick breathing exercise every two hours. This not only helps to reduce stress but also improves focus and productivity.

Consider the story of Jenna, a working woman constantly overwhelmed by workplace demands. She started incorporating the 4-7-8 breathing technique during her lunch breaks. Within weeks, she noticed a significant reduction in her anxiety levels and found it easier to delegate tasks without feeling the need to micromanage. Or think about Maria, a mother of three, who used deep-breathing exercises to calm herself during chaotic mornings. She would take a few minutes to practice box breathing before waking her kids. This simple practice helped her approach the morning rush with a sense of calm, making the whole routine smoother for everyone involved.

Time-Management Tips for a Balanced Life

Effective time management can be a game-changer in reducing the need for control. Managing your time well creates a sense of order and predictability, significantly decreasing anxiety. Poor time management, on the other hand, often leads to chaos and stress, which can trigger controlling behaviors. You might feel like you need to micromanage every detail to keep things from spiraling out of control. Improving your time management skills can create a more balanced and less stressful life.

Prioritization is a key strategy in managing your time effectively. Start by identifying what truly matters to you and focus your energy on those tasks. Make a list of your priorities and rank them in order of importance. This helps you allocate your time and resources more efficiently, ensuring you spend your energy on what truly matters. Time-blocking is another incredibly useful method. This involves dividing your day into blocks of time, each dedicated to a specific task or activity. By setting aside dedicated time for important tasks, you can work more efficiently and avoid the temptation to multitask, which often leads to mistakes and stress.

Several tools and apps can assist you in managing your time more effectively. Popular time-management apps like Trello and Asana offer visual ways to organize tasks and projects. You can create boards for different projects, set deadlines, and track your progress. Digital calendars like Google Calendar can also be incredibly useful. Use them to schedule your tasks, set reminders, and ensure that you allocate time for breaks and self-care. These tools help you stay on track and make it easier to manage your day without feeling overwhelmed.

Consider the case of Laura, a marketing manager who used to feel constantly overwhelmed by her workload. She started using Trello to organize her projects and tasks. She reduced her stress by breaking her to-do list into manageable chunks and setting realistic deadlines. She also used Google Calendar to schedule her tasks and set reminders for important deadlines. This structured approach allowed her to manage her work more efficiently, leaving more time for personal activities and reducing the need to control every detail.

Another example is Sarah, a mother of two who struggled to balance her household duties with her part-time job. She began using a digital calendar to schedule her day, setting aside specific times for work, household chores, and quality time with her children. By creating a structured yet flexible schedule, she managed her responsibilities more effectively, reducing her stress and improving her overall well-being. These examples show how better time management can help you create a more balanced and fulfilling life.

Creating Daily Routines for Flexibility

Establishing flexible routines can be a game-changer in managing control issues. Routines provide a sense of order and predictability, which can significantly reduce anxiety and stress. When you have a routine, you make fewer decisions throughout the day, which reduces decision fatigue. Imagine waking up and knowing exactly what your morning entails without thinking about it. This kind of structure helps to create a sense of stability and control from within rather than needing to control external circumstances.

To design a flexible daily routine, start with your mornings and evenings. Morning routines might include activities like a brief stretch, a healthy breakfast, and a few minutes of journaling or reading. Evening routines can involve winding down with a good book, a relaxing bath, or gentle yoga. The key is to choose activities that set a positive tone for your day and help you unwind at night. Integrate downtime into your schedule to ensure that you have moments to recharge. This can be as simple as a 15-minute coffee break in the afternoon or a short walk after lunch.

Life is unpredictable, and even the best-laid plans can go awry. Adapting routines to unexpected changes is crucial for maintaining flexibility. One effective strategy is to have backup plans in place. For example, if your morning workout gets canceled due to rain, have an indoor exercise routine ready. If a work meeting runs late, have a quick dinner option available to avoid further stress. The goal is to be prepared for disruptions without letting them derail your entire day.

Take the example of Karen, a project manager who used to feel overwhelmed by her packed schedule. She created a flexible work routine that included blocks of time for focused work, short breaks, and buffer periods for unexpected tasks. This approach allowed her to stay productive without feeling stressed. On the other hand, Marie, a mother of three, managed her family's hectic schedule by incorporating flexible routines. She set specific times for homework, play, and family dinners but left room for spontaneous activities. This reduced her stress and made her children feel more relaxed and happy.

Routines are not about rigidity but about creating a framework that supports your well-being. By designing flexible routines, you provide structure while leaving room for life's unpredictability. This balanced approach helps to reduce the need for control, allowing you to navigate your day with greater ease and calm.

Setting Realistic Expectations

Setting realistic expectations is crucial for reducing control behaviors. When you set the bar too high for yourself or others, it creates a constant sense of pressure and stress. Unrealistic expectations often lead to disappointment and frustration, making you feel like you must control everything to meet those lofty standards. This cycle can be exhausting and damaging to your mental health. On the other hand, realistic goal-setting can help you manage your time and energy more effectively, reducing the need for control and allowing you to focus on what truly matters.

The link between unrealistic expectations and stress is well-documented. When you expect perfection from yourself or others, you set yourself up for failure. This constant striving for an unattainable ideal can lead to chronic stress and anxiety. Setting realistic expectations can break this cycle and create a more balanced and fulfilling life. Realistic goals are achievable and provide a sense of accomplishment, boosting your self-esteem and reducing the need for control. They allow you to celebrate your successes without the constant fear of falling short.

One effective strategy for setting realistic goals is the SMART goals framework. SMART stands for Specific, Measurable, Achievable, Relevant, and Time-bound. For example, instead of setting a vague goal like "I want to get fit," a SMART goal would be "I will walk for 30 minutes, five days a week, for the next month." This goal is specific, measurable, achievable, relevant, and time-bound, making tracking your progress and staying motivated easier. Breaking down large tasks into smaller, manageable steps can make your goals more attainable. By focusing on one step at a time, you can avoid feeling overwhelmed and maintain a sense of control without being controlling.

Managing expectations in relationships is equally important. Honest conversations about expectations can help you and your partner understand each other's needs and limitations. Communicating openly and listening actively is essential, as well as showing empathy and understanding. Compromise and flexibility are key components of healthy relationships. You might have to adjust your expectations to accommodate your partner's needs, and they will likely do the same for you. Setting realistic expectations together can create a more supportive and balanced relationship.

Consider the story of Anna, a professional who set realistic career goals to manage her work-life balance. Instead of aiming for a promotion within a year, she focused on improving her skills and taking on challenging projects. This approach allowed her to grow professionally without overwhelming herself. Similarly, Jessica, a parent, set achievable family goals by involving her children. They created a weekly schedule that balanced school, extracurricular activities, and family time. This collaborative approach reduced Jessica's stress and made her children feel more involved and valued.

Setting realistic expectations can create a more balanced and fulfilling life. Whether it's in your career, relationships, or daily routines, realistic goals help you manage your time and energy effectively, reducing the need for control and allowing you to focus on what truly matters.

Quick Wins: Small Changes with Big Impact

Sometimes, making significant changes in your life can feel overwhelming. But what if I told you that small, incremental changes can lead to substantial improvements in reducing control behaviors? This concept is rooted in the Japanese philosophy of kaizen, which means continuous improvement. It's about taking small steps consistently to achieve long-term goals. When you start small, it's easier to maintain momentum and less daunting to implement. These tiny adjustments can accumulate over time, leading to significant positive changes in your life.

One of the benefits of starting small is that it reduces the pressure to be perfect. You don't have to overhaul your entire life in one go. Instead, you can focus on making minor adjustments that are manageable and sustainable. For instance, decluttering your workspace can provide an immediate sense of relief and order. A tidy environment can reduce stress and make it easier to focus on essential tasks. Practicing gratitude journaling is another simple change that can have a profound impact. By jotting down a few things you're grateful for each day, you shift your focus from what's wrong to what's right, fostering a more positive outlook.

Building on small successes is key to achieving larger goals. Making a small change and seeing the benefits creates a sense of accomplishment that motivates you to keep going. Celebrating these small wins is crucial. Whether treating yourself to a favorite snack or taking a short break to enjoy a hobby, acknowledging your progress reinforces positive behavior. Creating a habit loop can also help. This involves identifying a trigger, performing a small action, and rewarding yourself. Over time, this loop becomes ingrained, making it easier to maintain new habits.

Take the example of Rachel, a professional who felt overwhelmed by her workload. She started by decluttering her desk, which made her workspace more inviting and less stressful. This small change boosted her productivity, and she gradually implemented other minor adjustments, like scheduling short breaks and using a task management app. These small tweaks significantly improved her efficiency and reduced her need to control every detail.

Another example is Linda, a parent who struggled with managing her chaotic household. She began by establishing a simple morning routine for her family, which included a quick, five-minute tidy-up session. This minor adjustment reduced the morning rush and set a more positive tone for the day. Encouraged by this success, she made other small changes, like preparing lunches the night before and setting up a family calendar. These small steps collectively reduced her stress and improved the overall harmony at home.

Focusing on small, manageable changes can reduce control behaviors and create a more balanced life. These quick wins provide a sense of accomplishment and build momentum, leading to more significant improvements. Remember, it's not about making drastic changes overnight but about consistent, small steps that lead to lasting transformation.

In the next chapter, we'll explore how enhancing mental health and well-being can further support your efforts to relinquish control and embrace a more fulfilling life.

THREE

Enhancing Mental Health and Well-Being

Visualize yourself in a meeting at work, and suddenly, your mind starts racing. You worry about the presentation you have to give next week, the kids' soccer practice, and even whether you remembered to turn off the stove. Your heart pounds, your palms sweat, and you feel like you are losing control. This is anxiety, and it's a familiar foe for many of us. The good news is that there are powerful tools to manage these feelings, and Cognitive-Behavioral Therapy (CBT) is one of the most effective.

Cognitive-Behavioral Techniques for Anxiety

CBT is a type of therapy that focuses on changing unhelpful thought patterns and behaviors. It's based on the idea that our thoughts, feelings, and behaviors are interconnected. Identifying and altering negative thoughts can change how we feel and act. This therapy can be a game-changer for managing anxiety and reducing control issues.

At its core, CBT involves identifying cognitive distortions, which are irrational or exaggerated thoughts that fuel anxiety and control behaviors. Two common distortions are catastrophizing and black-and-white thinking. Catastrophizing involves imagining the worst possible outcome of a situation, making it seem far worse than it is. For example, if you make a mistake at work, you might think, "I'm going to get fired." On the other hand, black-and-white thinking involves seeing things in extremes—everything is either perfect or a disaster. You might believe everything will fall apart if you can't control every detail.

Cognitive restructuring is a key CBT technique that helps reframe these negative thoughts. Start by identifying a negative thought. Ask yourself what triggered it and how it makes you feel. Next, challenge the thought by examining the evidence for and against it. Is there a more balanced way to view the situation? Finally, replace the negative thought with a more positive or realistic one. For instance, instead of thinking, "I'm going to get fired," you might think, "Everyone makes mistakes; I can learn from this and improve."

Let's look at a real-life application. Consider Emily, a project manager who struggled with anxiety at work. She often felt overwhelmed by the need to control every aspect of her projects. Through CBT, Emily learned to identify her cognitive distortions. She realized she was catastrophizing and expecting perfection from herself and her team. By practicing cognitive restructuring, she challenged these thoughts and replaced them with more realistic ones. She started to see mistakes as opportunities for growth rather than disasters. This shift in mindset helped her reduce her anxiety and become a more effective leader.

Another example is Sarah, a mother who found it hard to relinquish control at home. She worried constantly about her children's safety and well-being, leading to overprotective behaviors. Through CBT, Sarah identified her black-and-white thinking. She believed something terrible would happen if she didn't oversee every detail. By challenging these thoughts and replacing them with more balanced ones, Sarah learned to trust her children's abilities and give them more independence. This not only reduced her anxiety but also improved her relationship with her kids.

CBT provides practical tools to manage anxiety and control issues. You can reframe your thoughts and change how you feel and act by identifying and challenging cognitive distortions. This empowers you to relinquish control and embrace a more balanced, fulfilling life.

Stress-Reduction Methods You Can Start Today

Managing stress is crucial for reducing control behaviors because chronic stress wreaks havoc on your mental health. When you're constantly stressed, your body is in a perpetual state of fight-or-flight, which can lead to anxiety, depression, and even physical health issues like high blood pressure. The link between stress and control is evident: the more stressed you are, the more you feel the need to control your surroundings to create a sense of stability. But this creates a vicious cycle, as the need for control often adds to your stress rather than alleviating it.

Chronic stress impacts your mental health in profound ways. It can make you feel constantly on edge, affect your concentration, and even alter your mood, making you more irritable and less patient. This means you're more likely to react impulsively, get overwhelmed easily, and resort to controlling behaviors to regain a sense of order. Understanding this connection is the first step toward breaking the cycle.

Simple stress-reduction techniques can make a significant difference. One effective method is progressive muscle relaxation. This involves tensing and slowly releasing each muscle group, starting from your toes and working your way up to your head. By focusing on the physical sensations, you can divert your mind from stressors and achieve a state of relaxation. Guided imagery is another powerful tool. Close your eyes and imagine yourself in a peaceful setting—like a beach or a forest. Engage all your senses to make the scene as vivid as possible. This mental escape can help lower your stress levels and give you a break from the pressures of daily life.

Incorporating stress reduction into your daily routines is easier than you think. Set aside dedicated time each day for relaxation activities. This could be as simple as a 10-minute meditation session in the morning or a short walk during your lunch break. Creating a stress-free environment at home also helps. Declutter your living space, play calming music, and use essential oils like lavender or chamomile to create a soothing atmosphere. These small changes can make your home a sanctuary where you can unwind and recharge.

Consider the story of Lisa, a marketing executive who felt overwhelmed by her demanding job. She started incorporating stress-reduction techniques into her workday, like taking short breaks to practice deep breathing and using guided imagery during lunch breaks. These small adjustments helped her manage her stress and improved her productivity. Similarly, Maria, a mother of two, used stress management techniques to improve her family dynamics. She introduced progressive muscle relaxation exercises before bedtime, turning them into a family activity. This reduced her stress and created a calming routine for her children, improving their sleep and overall mood.

By understanding the importance of stress management and incorporating simple yet effective techniques into your daily life, you can break the stress and control cycle and lead a more balanced and fulfilling life.

The Importance of Sleep and Rest

Quality sleep affects your mental health in profound ways. When you sleep well, your brain can restore and rejuvenate. This process is crucial for emotional regulation and overall mental well-being. On the flip side, poor sleep can exacerbate anxiety and make you feel more out of control. The next day feels like a battle on nights when you toss and turn. Your patience wears thin, and your ability to handle stress diminishes.

There's a strong connection between sleep and anxiety. When you're sleep-deprived, your body produces more cortisol, the stress hormone. Elevated cortisol levels can increase feelings of anxiety and make it harder to manage everyday stressors. Additionally, lack of sleep impairs your brain's ability to regulate emotions, leading to heightened irritability and mood swings. This emotional volatility can make you feel more out of control, perpetuating a cycle of anxiety and poor sleep.

Improving sleep quality can be a game-changer. Start by establishing a bedtime routine that signals your body it's time to wind down. This might include reading a book, taking a warm bath, or practicing gentle stretching. Consistency is key—try to go to bed and wake up at the same time every day, even on weekends. Creating a sleep-friendly environment also helps. Make sure your bedroom is cool, dark, and quiet. Consider using blackout curtains, earplugs, or a white noise machine to eliminate disruptions.

Common sleep issues can throw a wrench in your plans for better rest. Insomnia, characterized by difficulty falling or staying asleep, is a frequent culprit. If you struggle with insomnia, try relaxation techniques like progressive muscle relaxation or mindfulness meditation before bed. Another issue is sleep apnea, where breathing repeatedly stops and starts during sleep. If you suspect sleep apnea, consult a healthcare professional for proper diagnosis and treatment.

A CPAP machine or lifestyle changes like weight loss can make a significant difference.

Improved sleep can yield remarkable benefits. Take the story of Megan, who struggled with insomnia for years. She prioritized her sleep hygiene by establishing a consistent bedtime routine and calming environment. Within weeks, she noticed a significant reduction in her anxiety levels and felt more in control of her daily life. Another example is Jessica, a busy professional who balanced work and sleep. She used to burn the midnight oil, believing that sacrificing sleep was the only way to stay on top of her workload. After prioritizing sleep, she found that her productivity improved, and she was better equipped to handle stress.

Sleep is a powerful tool for enhancing mental health and reducing control behaviors. By prioritizing quality rest, you can improve emotional regulation, reduce anxiety, and create a more balanced, fulfilling life.

Nutrition and Its Impact on Mental Health

Imagine feeling more balanced and less anxious simply by adjusting what you eat. Nutrition profoundly affects your mental well-being and control behaviors. A balanced diet can stabilize mood, increase energy levels, and make it easier to manage stress. Specific nutrients play critical roles in mental health. For instance, omega-3 fatty acids, found in fish like salmon and walnuts, reduce symptoms of depression and anxiety. These nutrients help regulate neurotransmitters, chemicals in your brain that influence mood.

Incorporating a variety of fruits and vegetables into your diet is another powerful way to boost mental health. These foods are rich in antioxidants, vitamins, and minerals that support brain function. Leafy greens like spinach and kale are especially beneficial, as they contain folate, which helps produce neurotransmitters like serotonin and dopamine. These chemicals are often called the "feel-good" neurotransmitters because they help regulate mood and emotion. You can create a more stable and positive mental state by nourishing your brain with these essential nutrients.

While it's tempting to reach for sugary snacks or caffeinated beverages when you're stressed, these can exacerbate anxiety and control issues. Sugar can cause rapid spikes and drops in blood sugar levels, leading to mood swings and increased feelings of anxiety. High sugar consumption has also been linked to inflammation, negatively affecting brain function. Similarly, caffeine in coffee, tea, and many soft drinks can increase heart rate and make you feel jittery. For some, this heightened state of alertness can trigger anxiety and make it harder to manage stress.

Consider Jessica, a busy professional who used to rely on coffee and sugary snacks to get through her hectic days. She noticed that her anxiety levels were through the roof, and she was constantly on edge. After reading about the impact of diet on mental health, she decided to make some changes. Jessica started incorporating more omega-3-rich foods like salmon and walnuts into her meals. She also added a variety of colorful fruits and vegetables to her diet, focusing on leafy greens. Within weeks, she felt more balanced and less anxious. Her mood stabilized, and she found it easier to manage her workload without feeling overwhelmed.

Another example is Grace, a mother of two who struggled with mood swings and irritability. She realized her diet was high in sugar and caffeine, likely contributing to her emotional rollercoaster. Grace decided to cut back on sugary snacks and limit her caffeine intake. She replaced them with healthier options like fresh fruit, herbal teas, and whole grains. The change in her diet had a noticeable impact on her mental health. She felt more in control of her emotions and could handle the daily parenting challenges better.

By understanding the connection between diet and mental health, you can make informed choices that positively impact your well-being. Small changes in your eating habits can significantly improve mood, energy levels, and your ability to manage stress and anxiety.

Exercise as a Tool for Emotional Balance

Exercise is a potent ally in the quest for emotional balance and mental health. When you engage in physical activity, your body releases endorphins, often called "feel-good" hormones. These natural chemicals act as painkillers and mood elevators, reducing stress and fostering a sense of well-being. Regular exercise also helps lower cortisol levels. This dual action—boosting endorphins and reducing cortisol—creates a more balanced emotional state, making it easier to manage anxiety and control behaviors.

Incorporating exercise into your daily routine doesn't have to be a daunting task. Start with activities that you enjoy and can easily fit into your schedule. Walking, jogging, and cycling are excellent options that don't require special equipment or memberships. Yoga and Pilates are particularly beneficial for mental health as they combine physical movement with mindfulness and breathing techniques. Strength training and aerobic exercises also release endorphins and reduce stress. The key is finding a balance that works for you—mixing different exercises can keep things interesting and engage various muscle groups.

Finding time for exercise can be challenging, especially with a busy schedule. One common barrier is the lack of time. However, you can overcome this by breaking your exercise routine into shorter sessions spread throughout the day. Even a 10-minute walk during your lunch break or a quick yoga session in the morning can make a significant difference. Physical limitations can also pose a challenge. If you have mobility issues or chronic pain, consider low-impact exercises like swimming or chair yoga. The goal is to move in a way that feels good for your body and mind.

Real-life stories provide powerful motivation. Take the example of Rachel, a marketing executive who used exercise to manage her workplace stress. She started incorporating short, brisk walks during her breaks, gradually building up to longer weekend hikes. This simple change improved her physical health and helped her clear her mind and return to work with renewed focus. Another inspiring story is that of Lisa, a busy mother who found creative ways to include her kids in her exercise routine. She turned weekend park visits into family fitness sessions, where they would play games, run around, and even do yoga together. This helped Lisa manage her stress and fostered a healthy, active lifestyle for her children.

Exercise is a versatile tool that significantly enhances emotional balance and mental health. You can create a more balanced, fulfilling life by finding activities you enjoy, overcoming common barriers, and incorporating movement into your daily routine.

Incorporating Meditation into Your Daily Routine

Meditation is a practice that involves focusing your mind and eliminating distractions to achieve a state of relaxation and mental clarity. By dedicating time to meditating, you can significantly reduce anxiety and the urge to control everything around you. The beauty of meditation lies in its simplicity and the profound impact it can have on your mental health. It's a tool that helps you stay grounded, become more aware of your thoughts, and respond to life's challenges with a calm mind.

One of the most accessible forms of meditation is breathing meditation. Sit comfortably, close your eyes, and focus on your breath. Inhale deeply through your nose, hold for a moment, and then exhale slowly through your mouth. Pay attention to the sensation of the breath entering and leaving your body. If your mind wanders, gently bring your focus back to your breath. This practice helps center your thoughts and reduces stress by promoting relaxation.

Another effective technique is the body scan meditation. Lie down or sit comfortably, close your eyes, and take a few deep breaths. Starting from your toes, slowly move your attention up through your body, noticing any tension or discomfort. As you focus on each body part, consciously relax those muscles. This practice helps you become more in tune with your body and alleviates physical tension, contributing to overall mental well-being.

Making meditation a regular habit can be transformative. To integrate meditation into your daily routine, set a specific time each day for your practice. Consistency is key, whether first thing in the morning or right before bed. Creating a peaceful meditation space can also enhance your practice. Choose a quiet spot in your home where you feel comfortable and free from distractions. Adding elements like candles, soft lighting, or calming music can create a serene atmosphere that encourages relaxation.

Consider the story of Rebecca, a high-stakes lawyer who struggled with constant stress and anxiety. She began incorporating meditation into her daily routine, starting with just five minutes each morning. Over time, she extended her practice to 20 minutes, finding that it helped her manage work stress and improve her focus. Her colleagues even noticed a positive change in her demeanor and productivity. On the home front, Emily, a mother of three, introduced meditation to her children. They practiced together before bedtime, turning it into a calming family ritual. This improved Emily's mental health and created a peaceful bedtime routine for her kids, enhancing their emotional well-being.

Meditation offers a simple yet powerful way to reduce anxiety and manage control behaviors. Dedicating a few minutes daily to this practice can cultivate inner peace and resilience, allowing you to navigate life's challenges more easily. Whether you're a busy professional or a parent juggling multiple responsibilities, meditation can be a valuable addition to your mental health toolkit.

Enhancing mental health and well-being through these practices sets a solid foundation for personal growth. As we move forward, we'll delve into understanding control behaviors and how they manifest in various aspects of your life.

FOUR

Deep Self-Reflection and Awareness

Picture yourself sitting in a cozy nook with a cup of tea, a blank journal, and a pen poised to capture your thoughts. It's a quiet moment amidst the whirlwind of your busy life. This scenario might seem idyllic, but it's a powerful practice that can lead to profound self-discovery. Journaling is more than just putting pen to paper; it's a gateway to understanding your control behaviors and uncovering the root causes of your need for control.

Journaling enhances self-awareness by allowing you to explore your thoughts and feelings in a structured way. When you jot down your experiences, you gain clarity and insight into your behavior patterns. This process can help you identify triggers and understand why you react the way you do. Journaling also provides an emotional release, offering a safe space to express your frustrations, fears, and hopes. As you pour your thoughts onto the page, you lighten the mental load, making it easier to manage stress and control tendencies.

To get started, consider these guided journaling prompts designed to help you explore your control tendencies. First, describe a recent situation where you felt the need to control. What were your thoughts and feelings? Reflecting on specific instances can help you identify patterns and triggers. Next, ask yourself, "What are your biggest fears about losing control?" This question encourages you to dig deep and uncover the underlying anxieties that drive your need for control. By addressing these fears, you can begin to develop healthier coping mechanisms.

Different journaling techniques can keep the practice engaging and effective. Stream-of-consciousness writing is continuously writing without worrying about grammar or punctuation. This free-flowing style helps you tap into your subconscious mind, revealing thoughts and feelings you might not know. Gratitude journaling is another powerful technique. Each day, write down three things you're grateful for. Focusing on positive aspects of your life can shift your mindset from control and perfectionism to appreciation and contentment.

Consider the story of Laura, a professional who used journaling for emotional insight. Laura started journaling after feeling overwhelmed by her demanding job. Through her entries, she realized that her need to control every project stemmed from a fear of failure. By acknowledging this fear, Laura began to delegate tasks and trust her team, significantly reducing her stress levels. Another example is Jillian, a mother who felt pressured to be the perfect parent. Journaling helped her see that societal expectations drove her need for control. By recognizing this, Jillian learned to set realistic expectations for herself and her children, improving her relationship with them.

Guided Journaling Prompts:

1. Describe a recent situation where you felt the need to control. What were your thoughts and feelings?
2. What are your biggest fears related to losing control?

3. Write about a time when you let go of control, and things
    turned out better than expected.

Engaging in these practices can lead to significant personal growth
and emotional healing. By making journaling a regular part of your
routine, you can gain deeper insights into your behavior, reduce
anxiety, and foster a more balanced and fulfilling life.

Reflective Questions to Uncover Hidden Anxieties

Reflective questioning is a powerful tool for uncovering hidden
anxieties that drive your control behaviors. Asking yourself deep,
reflective questions can help you identify underlying fears and gain
insight into subconscious thoughts. These questions act as mirrors,
reflecting the hidden parts of your psyche that you might not be fully
aware of. This introspection aims to bring these hidden elements
into the light, allowing you to understand and address them.

One key benefit of reflective questioning is the identification of
underlying fears. For many of us, control behaviors are rooted in a
fear of uncertainty, failure, or inadequacy. By asking yourself targeted
questions, you can unearth these fears and understand how they
influence your actions. Another significant benefit is insight into
subconscious thoughts. Subconscious beliefs and patterns often
drive the need for control we might not recognize consciously.
Reflective questioning helps bring these hidden thoughts to the
surface, allowing you to examine them critically.

Consider asking yourself specific questions designed to prompt
introspection and reveal hidden anxieties. Start with, "What do you fear
might happen if you lose control?" This question encourages you to
confront your worst-case scenarios and examine the fears that drive your
need for control. Another powerful question is, "How does the need for
perfection impact your daily life?" Reflecting on this can help you

understand the toll perfectionism takes on your mental and emotional well-being. These questions are not about finding immediate solutions but gaining a deeper understanding of your inner world.

It is crucial to approach these questions honestly and thoughtfully. Take your time to reflect before writing your answers. Find a quiet space where you can be alone with your thoughts, free from distractions. Be honest with yourself and nonjudgmental. Remember, this is a safe space for exploration, not criticism. Allow yourself to feel any emotions and write them down without censoring yourself. This process can be uncomfortable, but it's a necessary step towards self-awareness and change.

Reflective questioning has led to significant breakthroughs for many individuals. Take the story of Shari, a mother who constantly needed to control every aspect of her children's lives. Through reflective questioning, she uncovered a deep-seated fear of inadequacy stemming from her childhood experiences. Recognizing this fear allowed Shari to let go of some of her control behaviors and trust her children more. Similarly, Jamie, a professional, struggled with a relentless need for perfection at work. Reflecting on the question, "What do you fear might happen if you lose control?" helped her realize that her fear of failure was driving her perfectionism. This insight enabled Jamie to set more realistic expectations and reduce her stress.

Reflective questioning is a journey into the depths of your psyche. By asking yourself the right questions and approaching them honestly and with compassion, you can uncover hidden anxieties and address the fears that drive your need for control. This process is not about finding immediate solutions but gaining a deeper understanding of your inner world. Through this self-awareness, you can make meaningful changes, reduce control behaviors, and foster a more balanced and fulfilling existence.

Understanding Your Triggers

Triggers are the emotional catalysts that drive our control behaviors, often without us even realizing it. An emotional trigger is any event or situation that evokes a strong emotional response, usually tied to past experiences or ingrained fears. Common triggers for control tendencies include unpredictable situations, relationships that challenge your sense of security, or even certain environments that remind you of past failures. Recognizing these triggers is crucial for managing control behaviors effectively.

To identify your triggers, start by keeping a trigger journal. Whenever you need to control a situation, jot down the specifics: What happened? How did you feel? What thoughts ran through your mind? Over time, patterns will emerge, helping you pinpoint what sets off your need for control. Note both your physical and emotional responses. Do you feel your heart rate increase? Do your thoughts race? These physical cues can be just as telling as your emotional reactions.

Once you've identified your triggers, managing them becomes the next step. Grounding techniques can be beneficial. These simple methods bring you back to the present moment, helping you regain control over your emotional state. One effective technique is the "5-4-3-2-1" method: Identify five things you can see, four things you can touch, three things you can hear, two things you can smell, and one thing you can taste. Another strategy is to develop a trigger action plan. This involves creating a step-by-step plan for how to respond when you encounter a trigger. For example, if a sudden change in plans sets you off, your action plan might include taking deep breaths, reminding yourself that things are okay to be imperfect, and then calmly addressing the change.

Real-life examples can illustrate how identifying and managing triggers can lead to significant improvements. Take the case of Emily, a professional who found that last-minute changes at work triggered her need to micromanage her team. By keeping a trigger journal, she realized that her anxiety stemmed from a fear of appearing incompetent. With this insight, she developed a trigger action plan that included grounding techniques and open communication with her team about her concerns. This approach reduced her stress and improved her relationships at work.

Another example is Terri, a parent who felt overwhelmed whenever her children's routines were disrupted. She noted her physical responses—tight chest and clenched fists—and used grounding techniques to calm herself. Terri also developed a trigger action plan, which included taking a moment to breathe, reassuring herself that flexibility is healthy for her children, and calmly addressing the situation. This strategy helped her manage her triggers more effectively, creating a more harmonious family environment.

By understanding and managing your triggers, you can gain control over your emotional responses rather than letting them control you. This reduces the urge to micromanage and over-control and fosters healthier relationships and a more balanced life.

The Role of Past Experiences

Our past experiences, especially childhood ones, can profoundly shape our control behaviors. Imagine growing up in an environment where unpredictability was the norm. Perhaps your parents were inconsistent in their rules, or maybe you faced trauma like neglect or abuse. These early experiences can create a deep-seated need for control to cope with uncertainty and fear. The influence of childhood trauma on your present behavior can be significant. If you were often left to fend for yourself or felt unsafe, you might have developed control behaviors as a survival mechanism. These patterns can persist into adulthood, affecting your relationships and daily life.

Past relationships also play a crucial role. Consider a previous relationship where you constantly felt undermined or invalidated. Such experiences can lead to an ingrained belief that you must control your environment to protect yourself. This is particularly true if you've had relationships that were emotionally or physically abusive. The impact of these past relationships can linger, making it difficult to trust others and let go of control. Reflecting on these experiences can provide valuable insights into why you may need to control situations and people in your current life.

To explore your past, write a timeline of significant life events. Note down moments that were particularly impactful, both positive and negative. Reflect on how these experiences shaped your need for control. Ask yourself questions like, "How did my childhood environment influence my behavior today?" or "What past relationships have contributed to my current need for control?" This exercise can help you connect the dots between your past and present, offering a clearer understanding of your behavior. Reflecting on past relationships and their impact can also be enlightening. Consider your interactions with significant people and how these relationships might have influenced your control tendencies.

Healing from past experiences involves several strategies. Seeking therapy or counseling can be incredibly beneficial. A trained professional can guide you through unpacking your past and developing healthier coping mechanisms. Therapy provides a safe space to explore your feelings and gain insights into your behavior. Practicing self-compassion and forgiveness is another crucial aspect of healing. Be kind to yourself as you reflect on your past. Understand that your control behaviors were likely developed to protect yourself. Forgive yourself for any perceived shortcomings and acknowledge your strength in seeking change.

Consider the story of Emma, a professional who grew up with a controlling parent. Emma realized that her need to control every detail at work stemmed from her childhood experiences. Through therapy, she learned to set boundaries and trust her team, significantly reducing her stress levels. Another example is Maria, a mother who faced childhood trauma. She often felt the need to micromanage her children's lives to ensure their safety. Through counseling and self-compassion, Maria learned to let go of her control tendencies and foster a more trusting relationship with her children.

Identifying Fear-Based Thoughts

Fear-based thoughts are those nagging voices in your head that stem from deep-seated anxieties and insecurities. They often arise from past experiences and can heavily influence your behavior, especially your need to control. These thoughts are usually negative, irrational, and exaggerated, making you feel like you must manage every little detail to prevent disaster. Characteristics of fear-based thinking include catastrophizing, where you always imagine the worst-case scenario, and black-and-white thinking, which makes you see situations in extremes.

Common fear-based thoughts related to control might include, "If I don't oversee this project, it will fail," or "If I don't plan every detail of this event, it will be a disaster." These thoughts create a sense of urgency and anxiety, driving you to micromanage situations. They can make you feel you must be perfect to avoid criticism or failure.

To identify these fear-based thoughts, start by keeping a thought journal. Write down your thoughts whenever you feel anxious or have the urge to control. Another helpful tool is a thought record worksheet, where you can document the situation, thoughts, emotions, and an alternative, more balanced thought. This exercise helps you see patterns in your thinking and understand the root of your anxiety.

The next step is challenging and reframing these thoughts. Cognitive restructuring techniques can be incredibly effective. Start by questioning the validity of your fear-based thoughts. Ask yourself, "Is this thought based on facts or assumptions?" and "What evidence do I have that supports or contradicts this thought?" Replace the negative thought with a more balanced one. For example, change "If I don't do it, it will fail" to "I can trust others to handle this task competently."

Positive affirmations can also help reframe your mindset. Create a list of affirmations that counteract your fear-based thoughts. For instance, if you often think, "I must be perfect to be valued," replace it with "I am worthy and valuable as I am." Repeat these affirmations daily to reinforce a more positive and balanced perspective.

Consider the story of Nora, a professional who constantly fears failure. She believed she would be seen as incompetent if she didn't control every aspect of her work. Nora identified and challenged her fear-based thoughts by keeping a thought journal and using cognitive restructuring. She replaced them with affirmations like, "I am competent and capable," which helped her delegate tasks and reduce her stress.

Another example is Grace, a parent who struggled with feelings of inadequacy. She feared her children would fail if she didn't control their activities. Through thought journaling and positive affirmations, Grace learned to trust her children's abilities, giving them more independence. This not only reduced her anxiety but also improved her relationship with her children.

Building Self-Awareness Through Reflection

Self-awareness is like a flashlight in a dark room—it illuminates those hidden corners of your mind where control behaviors often lurk. Understanding why you act as you do is the first step in making meaningful changes. When you're self-aware, you're better equipped to recognize your emotional triggers and understand the impact of your actions on yourself and others. This heightened awareness helps you regulate your emotions more effectively, reducing the need for control. Think about it: when you know what sets you off, you can take proactive steps to manage your reactions instead of letting them control you.

Increased self-awareness has numerous benefits. It enhances emotional regulation, making staying calm and composed in stressful situations easier. You become more empathetic, understanding your feelings and those of others. This improved empathy can lead to healthier relationships, as you're better able to navigate conflicts and communicate effectively. Additionally, self-awareness fosters personal growth by helping you identify areas for improvement and set realistic goals. It's like having a roadmap for your emotional and mental well-being.

To cultivate self-awareness, try incorporating reflective exercises into your routine. A daily reflection practice can be incredibly beneficial. At the end of each day, take a few minutes to think about your actions and emotions. Ask yourself questions like, "What triggered my need for control today?" and "How did I handle it?" Another powerful tool is mindfulness meditation. This practice involves focusing on the present moment and observing your thoughts and feelings without judgment. Over time, mindfulness can help you become more attuned to your inner world, making it easier to recognize and address control behaviors.

Integrating reflection into daily life doesn't have to be complicated. Set aside specific times for reflection, whether a few minutes each morning or a more extended session at the end of the week. Creating a reflection journal can also be helpful. Use it to jot down your thoughts, feelings, and insights as they arise. This practice helps you track your progress and provides a tangible record of your journey towards greater self-awareness. The key is consistency. Regular reflection lets you stay connected to your inner self, making recognizing and changing control behaviors easier.

Consider the story of Amelia, a professional who struggled with decision-making at work. By setting aside time for daily reflection, Amelia could identify patterns in her behavior. She realized her need for control stemmed from a fear of making mistakes. With this insight, Amelia began to trust her judgment more and delegate tasks to her team, improving her decision-making process and reducing her stress levels. Another example is Lindsay, a mother who used reflection to enhance her parenting. Through regular reflection, Lindsay noticed that her children's unpredictability triggered her control behaviors. By becoming more aware of her reactions, she learned to embrace flexibility, creating a more harmonious home environment.

Building self-awareness through reflection is a powerful way to reduce control behaviors and promote personal growth. By understanding your emotional triggers and recognizing the impact of your actions, you can make meaningful changes that lead to a more balanced, fulfilling life.

FIVE

Improving Relationship Dynamics

Visualize yourself sitting at the dinner table with your partner, but instead of enjoying the meal, you're mentally reviewing the day's events and what still needs to be done. You're so engrossed in your thoughts that you miss the subtle cues that your partner needs to talk. The silence stretches, and soon, both of you are feeling disconnected. This scenario is all too common, highlighting the critical role of effective communication in maintaining healthy relationships.

Effective Communication Skills

Clear communication is the bedrock of any strong relationship. When you communicate effectively, you reduce misunderstandings and build stronger connections with those around you. Clear and honest communication ensures you and your partner feel understood and valued. When you express your thoughts and emotions openly, it fosters an environment of trust and intimacy. Conversely, poor communication can lead to a breakdown in trust and create emotional distance. Misunderstandings can fester, turning minor issues into significant conflicts that strain your relationship.

So, how do you practice clear and honest communication? One essential technique is using "I" statements to express your feelings. Instead of saying, "You never listen to me," try, "I feel unheard when we talk." This approach focuses on your emotions rather than blaming your partner, making it easier for them to understand and empathize with your perspective. Balancing speaking and listening is equally important. Ensure you give your partner the space to express their thoughts and feelings without interruption. This balance creates a dialogue rather than a monologue, fostering mutual respect and understanding.

Non-verbal communication also plays a significant role in how your message is received. Your body language, facial expressions, and tone of voice can reinforce or contradict your words. For instance, crossing your arms while saying, "I'm not upset," sends mixed signals. Aligning your verbal and non-verbal messages is crucial for clear communication. Pay attention to your partner's non-verbal cues as well. Are they avoiding eye contact or clenching their fists? These signs can provide valuable insights into their emotional state, helping you respond empathetically.

To improve your communication skills, consider practicing active listening. This involves fully focusing on the speaker, understanding their message, and responding thoughtfully. A practical exercise is to have a conversation where you only listen and then paraphrase what your partner said to ensure you understood correctly. Another useful exercise is role-playing different communication scenarios. For example, practice discussing a common conflict with your partner and taking turns to express your feelings using "I" statements and active listening techniques. This practice can make real-life conversations smoother and more productive.

Effective communication involves speaking clearly, actively listening, and interpreting nonverbal cues. By practicing these skills, you can build stronger, more intimate relationships, reduce misunderstandings, and create a more harmonious environment in your personal and professional life.

Building Trust with Your Partner

Trust is the cornerstone of any healthy relationship. It's built on honesty, reliability, and emotional safety. When you trust your partner, you feel secure in the relationship, knowing they will be there for you, come what may. Consistency and reliability are crucial elements in building trust. When your partner consistently follows through on their promises, it reinforces the belief that they are dependable. This reliability forms the bedrock of trust, allowing you to feel safe and secure in the relationship. On the other hand, inconsistency and broken promises can erode trust, leaving you uncertain and anxious.

Vulnerability also plays a significant role in building trust. When you allow yourself to be vulnerable with your partner, you open up about your fears, insecurities, and dreams. This openness fosters a deeper connection, showing that you trust your partner enough to share your thoughts and feelings. This encourages your partner to be vulnerable with you, creating a cycle of mutual trust and understanding. The more you share, the stronger your bond becomes, paving the way for a more intimate and trusting relationship.

Rebuilding trust after it has been damaged requires patience and effort from both partners. One of the first steps is acknowledging mistakes and apologizing sincerely. A heartfelt apology shows that you recognize the hurt caused and are willing to make amends. It's important to be specific about what you're apologizing for and to express genuine remorse. Setting and respecting boundaries is another crucial step in rebuilding trust. Boundaries create a sense of safety and respect, making both partners feel secure. By clearly defining what is acceptable and what is not, you create a framework for rebuilding trust.

To foster mutual trust, practice transparency and openness. Share your thoughts and feelings honestly, without fear of judgment. This openness encourages your partner to do the same, creating a more authentic and trusting relationship. Engaging in trust-building activities together can also help strengthen your bond. Consider activities that require cooperation and mutual support, such as team sports, cooking a meal together, or embarking on a new hobby. These activities provide opportunities to demonstrate reliability and trustworthiness, reinforcing the trust in your relationship.

Take the story of Amy and Mark, a couple who faced a breach of trust when Mark was unfaithful. They decided to rebuild their relationship by attending couples therapy, where they learned to communicate openly and set clear boundaries. Mark consistently showed his commitment to change; over time, Amy began to trust him again. Another example is Wendy and Ed, who fostered trust through shared experiences. They started a new hobby together—gardening—which required teamwork and patience. Through this shared activity, they learned to rely on each other, strengthening their trust and deepening their bond.

Navigating Conflicts Without Control

Conflicts in relationships are as inevitable as the changing seasons. They arise from differences in perspectives, unmet needs, or even simple misunderstandings. While conflicts can be uncomfortable, they also offer opportunities for growth and deeper understanding. Imagine a scenario where you and your partner disagree on how to spend your weekend. You want to relax at home, while they prefer an outdoor adventure. This seemingly minor conflict can escalate if handled poorly. However, if approached with an open mind, it can lead to a compromise that satisfies both parties and strengthens your bond.

Financial disagreements, differing parenting styles, and unmet emotional needs are common sources of relationship conflict. These conflicts often stem from underlying issues such as stress, insecurity, or past experiences. Viewing conflicts as opportunities for understanding can shift your perspective. Instead of seeing them as threats, consider them chances to learn more about your partner's needs and values. This mindset can transform conflicts into constructive dialogues, fostering mutual respect and empathy.

When it comes to resolving conflicts, collaborative problem-solving techniques are invaluable. Start by identifying the issue and expressing your feelings without assigning blame. For instance, instead of saying, "You always spend too much money," try, "I feel anxious when our spending exceeds our budget." This approach opens the door to a more productive conversation. Next, brainstorm solutions together. Encourage each other to suggest possible compromises and evaluate them without judgment. The goal is to find a middle ground that works for both parties.

Using a calm and respectful tone during disagreements is crucial. Heated arguments often lead to hurtful words and emotional scars. Practice taking deep breaths and pausing before responding. This helps you stay grounded and prevents knee-jerk reactions. Recognize your emotional triggers and address them. If you feel your anger rising, step away from the conversation to cool down. This break can provide the clarity needed to continue the discussion with a clear mind.

Consider the story of Dorothy and Robert, who frequently clashed over household chores. Dorothy felt overwhelmed by the workload, while Robert believed he was contributing enough. Instead of letting the conflict fester, they decided to approach it collaboratively. They sat down and listed all the household tasks, then divided them based on their strengths and availability. This exercise not only resolved their conflict but also strengthened their partnership. Another example is Megan and Josh, who disagreed on how to discipline their children. By calmly discussing their concerns and finding a compromise, they created a consistent and effective approach to parenting.

Navigating conflicts without control involves emotional regulation and a willingness to understand your partner's perspective. By staying calm and open-minded, you can turn conflicts into opportunities for growth and deeper connection.

The Power of Active Listening

Active listening is a game-changer in any relationship. It means fully focusing on the speaker, understanding their message, and responding thoughtfully. Active listening goes beyond just hearing words; it involves paying attention to the speaker's emotions, body language, and underlying messages. When you practice active listening, you show your partner they are valued and understood, which is crucial for building trust and fostering a deep connection.

Characteristics of active listening include maintaining eye contact, nodding in acknowledgment, and responding with appropriate facial expressions. It also means avoiding interruptions and giving the speaker your undivided attention. These actions create a safe, open space where both partners feel heard and respected. The benefits of active listening are immense, as it builds trust, enhances understanding, and strengthens the emotional bond between partners.

To practice active listening, start with reflective listening and paraphrasing. When your partner speaks, reflect their words to them to show that you understand. For example, if they say, "I'm frustrated with work," you might respond, "It sounds like you're stressed about your job." This technique validates their feelings and encourages them to share more. Asking open-ended questions is another effective method. Instead of yes-or-no questions, ask ones that invite detailed responses, such as, "What do you think could help with your work stress?" This approach fosters a deeper conversation and shows genuine interest in their thoughts and feelings.

Listening barriers can hinder effective communication. Distractions and multitasking are common obstacles. You're not fully present if you're checking your phone or thinking about your to-do list while your partner is talking. Make a conscious effort to eliminate distractions and focus solely on the conversation. Prejudgments and assumptions are another barrier. You're less likely to listen openly if you enter a conversation with preconceived notions about what your partner will say. Approach each conversation with an open mind, ready to hear their perspective without judgment.

Try practical exercises like reflective listening with a partner to enhance your active listening skills. Take turns speaking and listening, practicing reflecting and paraphrasing each other's words. This exercise helps you become more attuned to your partner's emotions and messages. Role-playing different listening scenarios is another valuable practice. Create scenarios where one partner shares a concern and the other practices active listening techniques. This exercise can improve your ability to navigate real-life conversations and conflicts with empathy and understanding.

Active listening is a powerful tool that enhances communication and deepens connections in relationships. You can foster a more supportive and understanding relationship by practicing reflective listening, asking open-ended questions, and overcoming listening barriers. Remember, the goal is to hear the words, truly understand, and connect with your partner more deeply.

Setting Healthy Boundaries

Setting and respecting boundaries is the backbone of any healthy relationship. Boundaries define where one person ends and another begins, providing clarity and mutual respect. They act as invisible lines, protecting your emotional space and ensuring you feel safe and valued. When boundaries are respected, they foster emotional safety and trust, creating a relationship where both partners feel secure and understood. Without boundaries, relationships can become chaotic and stressful, leading to resentment and emotional burnout.

The connection between boundaries and respect is profound. When you establish clear boundaries, you communicate your needs and limits, which fosters mutual respect. Your partner understands what is acceptable and what is not, reducing misunderstandings and conflicts. This clarity helps build a foundation of trust, as both partners feel confident that their boundaries will be honored. Emotional safety is another critical aspect. Boundaries create a safe space to express yourself without fear of judgment or intrusion. This emotional safety is essential for deepening intimacy and connection.

To set effective boundaries, start by identifying your limits. Reflect on what makes you feel uncomfortable or stressed in your relationship. These feelings are often indicators of where boundaries are needed. Once you've identified your boundaries, communicate them assertively. Use clear and direct language to express your needs. For example, instead of saying, "I don't like it when you're late," try, "I feel anxious when you're late. Can we agree to communicate better about our schedules?" This approach emphasizes your feelings and needs, making it easier for your partner to understand and respect your boundaries.

Respecting others' boundaries is just as important as setting your own. One effective strategy is to listen and actively acknowledge your partner's needs. When they express a boundary, show that you understand and are willing to honor it. This might involve adjusting your behavior to ensure that their boundaries are respected. For instance, if your partner needs personal space after a long day, give them that time to unwind without interruption. Recognizing and respecting these boundaries demonstrates empathy and consideration, strengthening your relationship.

Consider the story of David and Jaimie, a couple struggling to maintain personal space. David loved socializing, while Jamie needed quiet time to recharge. They decided to set clear boundaries around their personal space. David agreed to give Jaimie an hour of solitude each evening while Jaimie committed to participating in weekend social activities. This compromise made both partners feel respected and understood, improving their relationship.

Another example is Crystal and Ricky, who set boundaries to manage their work-life balance. They established specific times for work and family activities, ensuring that neither aspect overshadowed the other. This balance helped them maintain harmony and reduced stress in their relationship.

Role-Playing Scenarios for Real-Life Practice

Role-playing can be a transformative tool for improving relationship dynamics. It offers a safe space to practice and refine your communication skills without the pressure of real-life consequences. Imagine being able to rehearse difficult conversations, such as discussing finances or addressing a recurring conflict, in a controlled environment. This practice allows you to experiment with different approaches and receive immediate feedback, helping you build confidence and competence. The beauty of role-playing lies in its ability to simulate real-life scenarios, allowing you to practice assertive communication, conflict resolution, and boundary-setting in a supportive setting.

Consider a scenario for practicing assertive communication. You and your partner can take turns playing the roles of speaker and listener. The speaker might express a common concern, such as feeling overwhelmed by household responsibilities. Using "I" statements, the speaker can say, "I feel stressed when I have to manage all the chores by myself." The listener's role is to practice active listening, reflecting on what they heard and acknowledging the speaker's feelings. This exercise helps both partners become more comfortable expressing and receiving honest, assertive communication.

Another valuable scenario involves resolving a common relationship conflict. For instance, you could role-play a disagreement about spending habits. One partner might express concerns about overspending, while the other responds defensively. Through role-playing, you can practice staying calm and focused on finding a solution rather than escalating the conflict. This might involve brainstorming compromises, such as setting a monthly budget or agreeing to discuss major purchases beforehand. You can develop more effective real-life strategies for navigating conflicts by rehearsing these scenarios.

To set up an effective role-playing session, establish clear roles and objectives. Decide who will play the speaker and the listener, and outline the specific scenario you want to practice. Each partner should have a clear understanding of their role and the goals of the exercise. After completing the role-play, debrief and reflect on the experience. Discuss what worked well and what could be improved. This reflection helps you identify strengths and areas for growth, making future interactions more productive.

Consider the example of Randi and Kevin, who used role-playing to enhance communication. They practiced discussing their differing parenting styles, with Randi expressing her preference for structure and Kevin advocating for more flexibility. By role-playing this conversation, they explored each other's perspectives and found a balanced approach that worked for both. Another example is Olivia and Kelsey, who practiced boundary-setting through role-play. They simulated a scenario where Olivia needed alone time after work, and Kelsey learned to respect her boundaries without feeling neglected. This practice strengthened their relationship by fostering mutual understanding and respect.

Role-playing is a powerful tool for improving relationship dynamics, offering a safe space to practice and refine your skills. Simulating real-life scenarios allows you to build confidence and competence in communication, conflict resolution, and boundary-setting. This practice enhances your relationship with your partner and equips you with the tools to navigate life's challenges more effectively.

In the next chapter, we'll explore strategies for balancing professional and personal life and provide you with practical tools to manage both spheres without feeling overwhelmed.

SIX

Balancing Professional and Personal Life

Imagine you're at your office, surrounded by many tasks—emails demanding immediate attention, a report due by noon, and a thirty-minute meeting. The laundry pile is towering at home, and the kids need help with homework. It feels like you're juggling flaming torches, desperately trying not to drop any. This chaotic scene is all too familiar for many, but what if you could use some productivity hacks to streamline your day and bring a sense of calm to your life?

Productivity Hacks for Busy Women

Productivity hacks are strategies or tools designed to help you work smarter, not harder. They are especially valuable for busy women juggling multiple roles. These hacks are all about making small adjustments that significantly improve how you manage your time and tasks. By increasing your productivity, you can reduce stress and free up more time for the things that matter most to you, whether it's spending time with your family, pursuing a hobby, or simply relaxing.

One of the most effective productivity hacks is using project management apps like Trello or Asana. These tools allow you to organize your tasks visually, set deadlines, and track progress. Trello uses boards, lists, and cards to help you manage projects flexibly and intuitively. You can create a board for each project and use cards to represent tasks. Asana offers similar functionalities but with more robust features for team collaboration. Both tools help you track what needs to be done, who's responsible, and when it's due, reducing the mental load of remembering everything.

Time-tracking tools like Toggl can also be a game-changer. Toggl allows you to track how much time you spend on different tasks, providing insights into where your time goes. This awareness can help you identify areas where you might be wasting time and make adjustments to be more efficient. By understanding your time usage, you can better allocate your time to high-priority tasks and minimize distractions.

Practical tips can make a world of difference in improving productivity. The Pomodoro Technique is a popular method where you work in focused intervals of 25 minutes, followed by a 5-minute break. After four intervals, take a longer break. This technique helps maintain concentration and prevents burnout. Another helpful tool is the Eisenhower Matrix, which helps you prioritize tasks based on urgency and importance. By categorizing tasks into four quadrants—urgent and important, important but not urgent, urgent but not important, and neither urgent nor important—you can focus on what truly matters and delegate or eliminate the rest.

Consider the story of Emily, a marketing manager constantly overwhelmed by her workload. She started using time-blocking, a technique for allocating specific blocks of time for different tasks. Emily used Trello to organize her projects and set up her calendar with dedicated time for focused work, meetings, and breaks. This approach helped her stay organized and reduced her stress significantly.

Another example is Sarah, a working mother who felt like she was drowning in responsibilities at work and home. She began using Toggl to track her time and identify where she could be more efficient. Sarah also implemented the Pomodoro Technique during work hours and used the Eisenhower Matrix to prioritize her tasks. These small changes helped her balance her professional and personal life more effectively, giving her more time to spend with her family and lessening her anxiety.

Productivity hacks offer practical solutions to streamline your day, making managing professional and personal responsibilities easier. Incorporating these tools and techniques can enhance productivity, reduce stress, and create more time for what truly matters.

Delegation Techniques for the Workplace

Delegation involves assigning tasks to others, which reduces control behaviors and prevents burnout. By sharing responsibilities, you lighten your workload and allow others to contribute their skills and strengths. This not only helps you manage your time better but also fosters a sense of teamwork and collaboration. When you delegate, you free up mental space, reducing the pressure to handle everything yourself. This shift can improve mental health, increase productivity, and a more balanced life.

Effective delegation begins with identifying tasks suitable for others to handle. Start by listing all your responsibilities and pinpointing which ones can be delegated. Consider repetitive, time-consuming tasks or benefit from a fresh perspective. Once you've identified these tasks, choose team members with the skills and capacity to handle them. It's essential to communicate clearly when delegating. Provide detailed instructions, set clear expectations, and establish deadlines.

Open communication helps ensure that everyone understands their roles and responsibilities, reducing the risk of misunderstandings and errors.

One common barrier to delegation is the fear of losing control. You might worry that tasks won't be completed to your standards or that mistakes will reflect poorly on you. To overcome this, start small. Delegate minor tasks and gradually increase their complexity as you build trust in your team. Another challenge is ensuring accountability. It's crucial to follow up on delegated tasks without micromanaging. Set regular check-ins to review progress and provide support if needed. This approach helps maintain accountability while giving team members the autonomy to complete their tasks.

Consider the example of Jessica, a project manager who struggled with delegation for years. She felt projects would fall apart if she didn't oversee every detail. Realizing her limitations, she started delegating smaller tasks to her team. She communicated expectations and set regular check-ins. Over time, she saw her team thrive, bringing new ideas and efficiencies to the projects—this improved team dynamics and allowed Jessica to focus on strategic planning and leadership.

Another inspiring story is that of Monica, a professional balancing multiple projects at a tech company. She felt overwhelmed by the sheer volume of work and realized that delegation was her only way out. She began by identifying tasks that her team members could handle more efficiently. Monica communicated clearly, setting expectations and providing necessary resources. As she delegated more, she noticed a significant improvement in her workload management. Her team felt more empowered, and Monica had more time to focus on high-priority tasks, leading to better overall performance.

Delegation is a powerful tool for managing your workload and improving team dynamics. By sharing responsibilities and trusting your team, you can reduce stress, prevent burnout, and create a more balanced professional life.

Reducing Workplace Stress

Workplace stress can feel like a constant companion, especially when juggling numerous responsibilities. One of the most common sources of stress is a high workload coupled with tight deadlines. When you're constantly racing against the clock, it can feel overwhelming, leading to anxiety and burnout. Another significant stressor is the need for more control over work processes. You may have brilliant ideas and strategies, but rigid structures or micromanagement can stifle your creativity and make you feel powerless.

To combat these stressors, practicing mindfulness at work can be incredibly effective. Mindfulness involves being present in the moment and paying attention to your thoughts and emotions without judgment. Even a few minutes of mindfulness practice can help calm your mind and reduce stress. Setting realistic goals and expectations is another crucial strategy. Break down large projects into smaller, manageable tasks and set achievable deadlines. This makes the workload seem less daunting and provides a sense of accomplishment as you complete each task.

Managing work-related anxiety often requires actionable techniques. Taking regular breaks to recharge is essential. Stepping away from your desk, even for a short walk or a quick stretch, can help clear your mind and reduce stress levels. During particularly stressful moments, relaxation techniques like deep breathing can make a difference. Close your eyes, take a few deep breaths, and focus on breathing. This simple act can help you regain your composure and approach your tasks with a clearer mind.

Consider the story of Lisa, a project manager who felt overwhelmed by her demanding job. She began incorporating deep-breathing exercises into her workday, taking a few minutes each hour to breathe deeply and relax. This small change significantly impacted her stress levels, helping her stay calm and focused. Another example is Maria, an employee who struggled with the chaos of her work environment. She started organizing her tasks and setting realistic goals. By planning her day and breaking down her tasks, Maria reduced her stress and increased her productivity.

These strategies provide practical solutions to manage workplace stress effectively, allowing you to maintain your mental health and improve your work performance.

Creating a Work-Life Balance Plan

Balancing professional and personal life is more than a desirable goal; it's crucial for your overall well-being. When you achieve a balanced life, you can enjoy the benefits of reduced stress, improved mental health, and better physical health. A balanced life allows you to be more present in both your professional and personal spheres, enhancing your relationships and overall satisfaction. On the flip side, an imbalance can lead to burnout, chronic stress, and a host of health issues. It can also strain your relationships, making it harder to connect with loved ones and enjoy your life fully.

Creating a work-life balance plan begins with assessing your current situation. Take a moment to reflect on how you spend your time and identify areas where you need to be more relaxed. Are you spending too many hours at work? Is your personal life suffering as a result? Setting clear boundaries is the next step once you pinpoint the areas needing improvement. This might mean establishing specific work hours and sticking to them or setting aside dedicated time for family and self-care. Boundaries help create a structure that supports balance and prevents work from encroaching on personal time and vice versa.

Maintaining a balanced life requires ongoing effort and practical strategies. Scheduling regular downtime is crucial. Whether it's a weekly yoga class, a daily walk, or simply time spent reading a book, these moments of self-care help recharge your batteries and keep stress at bay. Communicating your boundaries with colleagues and family is equally important. Tell your team you won't be available after a certain hour, and inform your family about your work commitments. Clear communication ensures everyone is on the same page and respects your need for balance.

Consider the story of Anna, a software engineer who felt overwhelmed by her demanding job. She implemented a flexible work schedule that allowed her to work from home two days a week. This change gave her more time to spend with her young children and reduced her commute stress. She also set clear boundaries with her team, letting them know her availability and sticking to it. This plan not only improved her work performance but also enhanced her overall well-being.

Another example is Melissa, a marketing executive and mother of two. She prioritized family time through structured planning. She set aside an hour for family dinners every evening, followed by a no-work policy until the kids went to bed. She also scheduled regular date nights and solo weekend self-care activities with her partner. This structured approach helped Melissa balance her professional and personal responsibilities, leading to a more fulfilling and less stressful existence.

Managing Perfectionism at Work

Perfectionism in the workplace can be a double-edged sword. On one hand, it drives you to produce high-quality work. On the other, it can be a relentless taskmaster. Setting unrealistic standards often leads to burnout. You push yourself to the brink, striving for flawlessness in every project. This constant pressure can cause mental and physical exhaustion, making it difficult to sustain productivity over time.

The impact of perfectionism doesn't stop with you. It extends to your team and colleagues. You might expect the same from others when you hold yourself to impossibly high standards. This can create a tense work environment where no one feels good enough. Collaboration suffers because team members might shy away from contributing, fearing criticism or rejection. The stress of trying to meet these high expectations can stifle creativity and innovation, turning the workplace into a pressure cooker.

To manage perfectionism, start by setting realistic and achievable goals. Break larger projects into smaller, manageable tasks with clear, attainable objectives. This helps you stay focused and reduces the overwhelming feeling that everything must be perfect. Embrace the concept of "good enough." Understand that perfection isn't always necessary and that sometimes, good enough is perfectly acceptable. This mindset allows you to complete tasks more efficiently without getting bogged down by unnecessary details.

Adopting a growth mindset can also be a powerful way to combat perfectionism. Instead of seeing mistakes as failures, view them as learning opportunities. This shift in perspective encourages continuous improvement and reduces the fear of making errors. Focus on progress rather than perfection. Celebrate small victories and acknowledge the effort you put into your work, even if it's not flawless. This approach helps you build resilience and maintain a healthier work-life balance.

Take the example of Laura, a marketing director who struggled with perfectionism. She realized that her need for everything to be perfect was causing her immense stress and affecting her team. Laura began setting more realistic goals and embraced the "good enough" mindset. She also encouraged her team to share ideas without fear of criticism. This change fostered a more collaborative environment and improved overall productivity.

Another inspiring story is that of Teresa, an engineer who always aimed for perfection in her projects. This often led to delays and burnout. Teresa decided to focus on progress instead of perfection. She set achievable milestones and celebrated each one. This not only reduced her stress but also improved her performance. Her team noticed the positive change and followed her lead, creating a more supportive and productive work environment.

Relaxation Methods for Busy Schedules

Incorporating relaxation techniques into your daily routine is crucial for maintaining mental health, especially when juggling multiple roles and responsibilities. Regular relaxation helps to reduce stress, improve mood, and increase overall well-being. When you make time to relax, you're giving your mind and body a chance to reset, which can significantly reduce anxiety and the urge to control every detail of your life. This downtime isn't a luxury; it's necessary for anyone seeking balance and fulfillment.

The benefits of regular relaxation are numerous. It helps lower your heart rate and blood pressure, reduces muscle tension, and alleviates symptoms of anxiety and depression. When you take the time to relax, you also improve your focus and productivity, as a relaxed mind is better equipped to handle tasks efficiently. Moreover, incorporating relaxation into your routine can enhance your relationships by making you more present and less irritable.

Quick and easy relaxation techniques can be integrated into even the busiest schedules. A five-minute meditation session can work wonders. Find a quiet spot, close your eyes, and focus on your breath. Let your thoughts come and go without judgment. This brief practice can calm your mind and help you feel centered. Stretching exercises at your desk are another simple way to relax. Reach your arms above your head, roll your shoulders, and stretch your neck. These movements can relieve physical tension and refresh your mind.

Incorporating relaxation into your daily routine doesn't have to be complicated. Schedule short relaxation breaks throughout your day. Set a timer to remind yourself to take a five-minute break every hour. Use this time to stretch, breathe deeply, or simply close your eyes and relax. Creating a calming evening routine can also make a significant difference. Dim the lights, play soft music, and engage in activities that help you unwind, such as reading a book or taking a warm bath. This routine signals your body that it's time to relax and prepare for restful sleep.

Consider Emily, a busy lawyer who felt constantly on edge. She started incorporating short meditation sessions during her work breaks. Five minutes of focused breathing helped her manage stress and improve her concentration. Another example is Lisa, a working mother of two. She introduced her children to simple relaxation techniques like deep breathing and gentle stretching before bedtime. This practice helped her relax and created a calming routine for her kids, improving their sleep and overall mood.

Integrating relaxation methods into your busy schedule is a practical way to reduce stress and improve well-being. These techniques are simple yet effective, making it easier to navigate the demands of daily life with a calm and balanced mind.

Balancing professional and personal life requires a combination of effective strategies and practical tools. You can achieve a more fulfilling and less stressful life by incorporating relaxation methods, managing perfectionism, and creating a work-life balance plan. In the next chapter, we'll explore how to build a support network to enhance your well-being further.

SEVEN

Managing Technology and Digital Distractions

Envision you're at your desk, intending to finish that important report before lunch. Your phone buzzes with a notification—another email or a social media alert. You glance at it, thinking it'll just take a second, but soon, you find yourself scrolling through your feed, watching cute cat videos, and reading articles you didn't plan on. Before you know it, an hour has slipped by, and you're left feeling guilty and more stressed than before. While incredibly useful, technology can be a double-edged sword, especially when managing control behaviors.

Impact of Technology on Control Behaviors

Technology has become integral to our lives, weaving into nearly every aspect of our daily routines. From smartphones and laptops to smart home devices, technology provides convenience and efficiency. However, it also has a significant impact on our control behaviors. On one hand, technology can exacerbate the need for control. The constant flow of information and the pressure to stay connected can create a sense of urgency and anxiety. You might feel compelled to check your emails every few minutes or respond to every notification immediately, believing that staying on top of things will help you maintain control. This constant connectivity can lead to hypervigilance, where you're always on alert, ready to react to the next digital disruption.

On the other hand, technology can also be a powerful tool for managing control behaviors. Various apps and tools are designed to help you organize your tasks, set reminders, and manage your time effectively. For instance, project management apps like Trello and Asana allow you to visualize your tasks, set deadlines, and track your progress. These tools can help you plan and execute your responsibilities without feeling overwhelmed. Additionally, digital calendars like Google Calendar can help you schedule your day, set reminders, and allocate time for breaks and self-care. Using technology mindfully, you can create a sense of structure and order, reducing the need to control every detail manually.

However, the effects of constant connectivity and digital distractions on mental health cannot be ignored. The barrage of notifications, emails, and social media updates can create a constant distraction, making it difficult to focus on tasks and decreasing productivity. This can exacerbate feelings of anxiety and stress as you struggle to manage your responsibilities amidst the digital noise. The fear of missing out (FOMO) can further fuel this anxiety, making you feel compelled to stay connected and up-to-date with everything happening around you. This constant state of alertness can take a toll on your mental health, leading to burnout and emotional exhaustion.

Consider the story of Emma, a marketing executive constantly overwhelmed by work and personal responsibilities. She always kept her phone by her side, checking emails and messages even during family dinners. This constant connectivity made her feel stressed and anxious as she struggled to balance her work and personal life. Realizing the impact on her mental health, Emma decided to make some changes. She set specific times during the day to check her emails and turned off non-essential notifications. She also used a digital calendar to schedule her tasks and allocate time for breaks. These small adjustments helped her regain control without feeling overwhelmed by technology.

Another example is Sarah, a mother of two who struggled with the pressure to stay connected through social media. She constantly compared her life to others, feeling inadequate and stressed. To address this, Sarah decided to take a digital detox, limiting her social media usage to specific times of the day. She also unfollowed accounts that triggered negative feelings and started following pages that promoted positivity and self-care. This mindful approach to technology helped Sarah reduce her anxiety and focus on what truly mattered in her life.

While technology can contribute to control behaviors, it can also be leveraged as a tool for better management. The key is to use it mindfully and purposefully, setting boundaries and creating a balance that works for you. By understanding the impact of technology on your mental health and control behaviors, you can make informed choices that enhance your well-being and productivity.

Reflection Exercise: Assess Your Technology Habits

Take a moment to reflect on your relationship with technology. Consider the following questions:

1. How often do you check your phone or email during the day?
2. Do you feel anxious or stressed when you're not connected or up-to-date with notifications?
3. How does constant connectivity affect your productivity and mental health?

4. Are there specific apps or tools that help you manage your tasks and responsibilities effectively?
5. What changes can you make to use technology more mindfully and reduce digital distractions?

Write down your thoughts and observations in a journal. Identifying your habits and their impact on your life is the first step towards making positive changes. Remember, the goal is to create a balanced and mindful approach to technology that supports your well-being and helps you manage control behaviors effectively.

Technology can be a source of stress and a tool for better management. By understanding its impact on your control behaviors and mental health, you can make informed choices that enhance your well-being and productivity. Use technology mindfully, set boundaries, and create a balance that works for you. This approach will help you reclaim control without feeling overwhelmed by the digital world.

Strategies for Healthy Technology Use

You know that feeling when you've spent hours scrolling through social media or answering emails and suddenly realize the whole evening has slipped away? It's easy to let technology take over our lives without even noticing. The key to healthy technology use lies in setting boundaries. One effective way to do this is by establishing screen time limits. For instance, you might decide that after 8 PM, your phone goes on "Do Not Disturb" mode. This simple boundary can free up your evenings for activities that enrich your life, like spending quality time with family or diving into a good book.

Digital detoxes are another powerful tool. These are periods when you intentionally disconnect from all digital devices. It might be a full day over the weekend or just a few hours each evening. The goal is to create a space where you can recharge without the constant buzz of notifications. During a digital detox, you could engage in activities that ground you—like taking a walk, cooking a meal from scratch, or engaging in a hobby. It's about finding joy and relaxation in the real world, away from screens. Think of it as a mini-vacation for your mind.

Mindful and purposeful use of technology is essential for maintaining a healthy relationship with your devices. Start by being intentional about when and why you're using technology. Before opening an app or checking your phone, ask yourself if it's necessary. Are you reaching for your phone out of habit or boredom? If so, consider what else you could do that would be more fulfilling. Set specific times for checking emails and social media rather than constantly being available. This helps you stay focused and reduces the anxiety of being perpetually connected.

Creating designated tech-free zones in your home can also help. For example, make the dining room where phones are not allowed. This encourages meaningful conversations during meals and fosters a stronger connection with your loved ones. The bedroom is another great tech-free zone. Removing electronic devices from your sleeping area can improve the quality of your sleep and make your bedroom a sanctuary for rest. Invest in an old-fashioned alarm clock to wake you up instead of relying on your phone, which can tempt you to check messages and notifications first thing in the morning.

Another strategy is to customize your notifications. Not all notifications are created equal; some are more disruptive than others. Go through your phone settings and disable non-essential notifications. Do you need to know every time someone likes your photo or comments on a post? Limiting notifications to only the most important ones can significantly reduce digital distractions. This helps you stay focused on the task and reduces the urge to check your phone constantly.

Being mindful about the content you consume is equally important. Curate your social media feeds to include accounts that inspire and uplift you. Unfollow or mute pages that trigger stress, anxiety, or negative feelings. Social media should be a source of joy and connection, not a breeding ground for comparison and self-doubt. Follow pages that align with your interests and values, and engage with content that enriches your life. This simple act of curating your feed can transform your social media experience from draining to empowering.

Consider implementing tech-free times in your daily routine. For instance, try starting your day without immediately reaching for your phone. Instead, spend the first 30 minutes doing something that sets a positive tone for the day, like stretching, meditating, or journaling. The same goes for the end of the day. Power down your devices at least an hour before bed and engage in calming activities that help you wind down. This can improve your sleep quality and overall mental well-being.

Another helpful practice is the "one-screen rule." This means using only one screen at a time. If you're watching a movie, put your phone away. If you're working on your computer, close unnecessary tabs and avoid checking your phone. This not only helps you stay focused but also allows you to immerse yourself fully in the activity at hand. It's about being present and mindful rather than letting technology simultaneously pull you in multiple directions.

To make these strategies more effective, involve your family or household members. Create a family tech plan where everyone agrees on specific rules and boundaries around technology use. This could include tech-free family dinners, weekend digital detoxes, or setting screen time limits for children. By involving everyone, you create a supportive environment that makes it easier to stick to these boundaries and encourages healthier technology habits for the entire family.

Let's not forget about the importance of regular breaks. The Pomodoro Technique, which involves working for 25 minutes and then taking a 5-minute break, can be incredibly effective. Use these breaks to step away from screens and do something refreshing, like stretching, grabbing a glass of water, or simply looking out the window. These short breaks can prevent burnout and keep your mind sharp, making you more productive and focused.

Lastly, consider the benefits of analog activities. Sometimes, the best way to reduce screen time is to replace it with something equally engaging but non-digital. Pick up a new hobby like crocheting, painting, or gardening. Read a physical book instead of an e-book. Write in a journal instead of typing on a computer. These activities can be incredibly fulfilling and provide a much-needed break from the constant stimulation of digital devices.

Balancing Technology and Real-Life Interactions

Think about the last time you were out with friends and noticed that everyone, including yourself, was more engaged with their phones than with each other. It's a common scene where digital interactions overshadow face-to-face conversations, neglecting real-life connections. In today's world, balancing technology and real-life interactions is more important than ever. While technology offers countless benefits, it can also disrupt meaningful relationships if not managed carefully.

Human interactions are the cornerstone of emotional well-being. When you connect with someone face-to-face, you engage in a rich exchange of verbal and non-verbal cues that simply can't be replicated through a screen. Eye contact, body language, and even the tone of voice contribute to a deeper understanding and emotional connection. These interactions help build trust, empathy, and a sense of belonging, all crucial for mental health. When technology takes precedence over these real-life moments, it can create a sense of isolation and disconnection. You might feel lonely even when you're "connected" to hundreds of people online.

It's also worth noting that real-life interactions offer an opportunity for spontaneous and genuine moments that digital communication often lacks. Think about the joy of a surprise visit from a friend or the shared laughter over an unexpected joke during a conversation. These moments enrich our lives and contribute to our overall happiness. When constantly distracted by your phone or other devices, you miss out on these priceless experiences. Balancing technology with real-life interactions means being present at the moment and fully engaging with the people around you.

Creating tech-free zones and times in your daily routine can be a game-changer. For instance, designate the dining table as a no-phone zone. This simple rule encourages everyone to engage in meaningful conversations during meals. You might learn more about your partner's day, your children's thoughts, or your friends' experiences. These conversations can strengthen your relationships and provide a sense of connection that no amount of digital interaction can replace. Similarly, consider setting aside specific times in the day when you put away your devices. Whether during your morning coffee, evening walk, or bedtime routine, these tech-free moments allow you to focus on yourself and the people around you.

Remember the importance of engaging in activities that limit your screen time while fostering real-life connections. Joining a local club, attending community events, or participating in group activities like sports or book clubs can help you build new relationships and strengthen existing ones. These activities offer a break from the digital world and provide opportunities for face-to-face interactions. They also allow you to pursue interests and hobbies that bring joy and fulfillment, contributing to a balanced and enriching life.

Consider the impact of technology on family dynamics. Children, in particular, are highly influenced by the behavior of adults around them. If they see you constantly glued to your phone, they will likely mimic that behavior. Setting a good example by balancing your screen time can encourage healthier habits in your children. Engage in family activities that don't involve screens, like board games, outdoor adventures, or cooking together. These activities strengthen family bonds and create lasting memories that digital interactions can't offer.

Balancing technology with real-life interactions can enhance your work relationships and overall job satisfaction. While emails and instant messages are convenient, they can't replace the value of face-to-face meetings and discussions. Opt for in-person meetings or video calls that allow for more personal interaction whenever possible. These conversations can lead to better understanding, increased collaboration, and stronger professional relationships. They also enable spontaneous brainstorming and problem-solving, which can be more challenging through digital communication.

One practical approach to balancing technology and real-life interactions is being intentional about digital consumption. Before reaching for your phone or opening a social media app, ask yourself if it's necessary or if there's a more fulfilling activity you could engage in. This mindfulness can help you make more conscious choices about your time. It can also reduce the feeling of being overwhelmed by digital distractions, allowing you to focus on what truly matters.

Another strategy is to use technology to enhance rather than replace real-life interactions. For example, use social media to plan and organize get-togethers with friends or family. Share photos and updates to stay connected, but don't let it substitute for face-to-face interactions. Technology can be a great tool for maintaining relationships, but there are other ways to connect with others. Prioritize in-person meetings and experiences whenever possible, and use digital tools as a supplement rather than a replacement.

Balancing technology and real-life interactions is crucial for maintaining healthy relationships, reducing stress, and enhancing overall well-being. You can create a more balanced and fulfilling life by being mindful of your digital consumption, creating tech-free zones and times, and prioritizing face-to-face interactions. Remember, the goal is not to eliminate technology but to use it to support and enhance your real-life connections.

As we move forward, we'll explore how to build a support network to enhance your well-being further and help you navigate the challenges of balancing your professional and personal life.

EIGHT

Parenting Without Control

Picture for a moment that you're at the park, watching your child play on the swings. You notice another parent hovering closely, directing every move their child makes. They try to ensure everything goes perfectly, but the child's frustration grows. This scene is all too common, underscoring the importance of setting healthy boundaries. As parents, the urge to control every aspect of our children's lives can be strong, but stepping back and allowing them to grow independently is crucial.

Setting Healthy Boundaries with Children

Establishing boundaries with your children is essential for fostering respect and understanding in your relationship. Boundaries help children learn what is acceptable and what isn't, promoting a sense of security and stability. They also teach children self-discipline, a vital skill for navigating the complexities of life. When boundaries are clear and consistently enforced, children understand the expectations and feel more confident in their actions.

Let's discuss how to establish these boundaries. Start by setting age-appropriate limits. This might mean simple rules for younger children, like putting toys away after playtime. For teenagers, boundaries could include curfews and guidelines for social media use. The key is ensuring these boundaries are relevant to their developmental stage and capabilities.

Consistency is crucial when it comes to enforcing rules. If a boundary is set, it must be upheld each time the situation arises. Inconsistency can confuse children and undermine the boundary's effectiveness. For example, if screen time is limited to one hour daily, this rule should be consistently applied. Exceptions can be made for special occasions, but they should be communicated and understood as rare.

Communicating boundaries effectively is just as important as setting them. Use positive language when explaining rules to your children. Instead of saying, "Don't leave your toys out," try, "Please put your toys away when you're done playing." Positive language focuses on desired behaviors rather than prohibiting actions, making it easier for children to understand and follow the rules.

Involving your children in setting these boundaries can also be beneficial. When children participate in creating rules, they are more likely to understand and respect them. For instance, if you're setting limits on screen time, discuss with your child what they think is a reasonable amount and why. This collaborative approach fosters a sense of ownership and responsibility.

Here are some specific examples of healthy boundaries. Setting screen time limits can prevent overuse and promote a balanced lifestyle. For instance, you might allow one hour of screen time on weekdays and two hours on weekends. Bedtime routines are another area where boundaries are essential. A consistent bedtime helps children get the rest they need and creates a sense of predictability. You might set a rule that lights go out at 8 PM, with a calming bedtime routine leading up to it.

Reflect and Implement

Take a moment to consider the boundaries you currently have for your children. Are they age-appropriate and consistently enforced? Reflect on how you communicate these rules and how your children respond. Make a list of any areas where boundaries could be improved or added. Discuss these with your children and involve them in setting new limits.

The next section will explore how encouraging independence can further support your child's growth and development.

Encouraging Independence in Kids

Encouraging independence in your children is one of the most empowering gifts you can offer them. It builds self-confidence and teaches them invaluable problem-solving skills. When children learn to navigate challenges independently, they develop a sense of capability and resilience. Independence also fosters a sense of responsibility, helping them understand the consequences of their actions and decisions.

One effective strategy for encouraging autonomy is allowing your children to make choices. Start with simple decisions, such as choosing their clothes for the day or selecting a healthy snack. As they age, you can expand their choices to more significant decisions, like planning a family outing or managing their allowance. This empowers them and teaches them the importance of making thoughtful decisions.

Encouraging self-help skills is another crucial aspect. Teach your children to manage basic tasks independently, like tying their shoes, packing their school bags, or preparing a simple meal. These small steps build their confidence and competence, showing them they can care for themselves. It's essential to offer guidance initially but gradually step back as they become more proficient. This balance between support and freedom is key to fostering independence without overwhelming them.

Knowing when to step back is an art in itself. It's natural to want to step in and help when you see your child struggling, but sometimes, letting them work through challenges independently is more beneficial. This doesn't mean abandoning them; instead, it's about offering support without taking over. For example, if your child is working on a homework assignment, resist the urge to correct every mistake immediately. Instead, provide guidance and encourage them to find solutions independently when asked.

Real-life examples can illustrate how powerful these strategies can be. Take the story of Olivia, a five-year-old who loves picking out her clothes each morning. Her parents noticed that allowing her this choice made her more excited about getting dressed and ready for school. It also reduced morning conflicts, as Olivia felt more in control of her routine. Then there's Sam, a ten-year-old who manages his homework schedule. His parents gave him the responsibility of deciding when to do his assignments, with the understanding that all work must be completed by bedtime. Sam learned to prioritize tasks and manage his time effectively, which will benefit him in the long run.

Encouraging independence is about striking a balance. It's about providing the right amount of guidance while allowing your child the freedom to explore and learn from their experiences. This balance helps them grow into confident, capable individuals who trust their abilities and judgment. By fostering independence, you're not just preparing them for the challenges of today but also equipping them for the uncertainties of tomorrow.

Positive Reinforcement Techniques

Positive reinforcement is a powerful parenting tool that rewards desirable behaviors and encourages repetition. Unlike punishment, which aims to stop unwanted actions, positive reinforcement strengthens good behavior by providing a motivational boost. At its core, positive reinforcement involves adding a pleasant consequence immediately after a behavior occurs, making the behavior more likely to be repeated. This approach improves behavior and boosts children's self-esteem and confidence, fostering a more positive and nurturing environment.

One effective method for using positive reinforcement is praising effort and progress rather than just outcomes. For example, if your child spends time studying for a test, praise their dedication and hard work, regardless of the final grade. This reinforcement emphasizes the value of effort and perseverance, teaching children that the process is just as important as the result. It helps them understand that their hard work is noticed and appreciated, motivating them to continue putting in effort.

Using reward systems can also be an effective way to reinforce positive behavior. Create a simple chart where your child can earn stickers or points for completing tasks or displaying good behavior. Once they accumulate certain stickers or points, they can trade them in for a reward, such as extra playtime or a special outing. This system provides a clear and tangible way for children to see the benefits of their positive actions, making it more likely that they will continue to behave well.

However, it's crucial to avoid common pitfalls when using positive reinforcement. Over-reliance on material rewards can backfire, as children may start to expect a tangible reward for every good deed, diminishing intrinsic motivation. To counter this, mix material rewards with non-material ones, such as verbal praise, extra playtime, or a special activity. Inconsistent application is another common mistake. If you only occasionally reinforce positive behavior, the effectiveness of the reinforcement diminishes. Ensure that you consistently acknowledge and reward desirable behaviors to maintain their impact.

Consider the story of Ava, who used positive reinforcement to encourage her son to complete his chores. Instead of simply telling him to clean his room, she praised his efforts each time he made progress, no matter how small. Over time, her son began to take pride in his tidy space and needed less prompting to keep it clean. Similarly, Lisa used a reward system to encourage her daughter to practice the piano regularly. By earning points for each practice session, her daughter felt motivated and looked forward to her practice time, leading to noticeable improvement in her skills.

Positive reinforcement can be a game-changer in parenting. It encourages desirable behavior and fosters a supportive and positive environment where children feel valued and motivated. By praising effort, using reward systems wisely, and avoiding common pitfalls, you can effectively harness the power of positive reinforcement to enhance your child's development and create a happier, more harmonious home.

Creating a Nurturing Home Environment

Creating a nurturing home environment is more than just providing physical comfort; it fosters emotional safety and support. A nurturing home is where everyone feels valued, loved, and encouraged. It's a place where children can express themselves without fear of judgment, knowing they have a safe space to return to no matter what. Emotional safety means children feel secure enough to share their feelings and thoughts openly. Support means being there for them, offering guidance and encouragement, and celebrating their successes while helping them navigate their failures.

To cultivate such an environment, start by establishing family rituals. These rituals, whether as simple as a weekly movie night or as elaborate as holiday traditions, create a sense of belonging and stability. They offer regular opportunities for family members to connect and bond. For instance, having Sunday dinners where everyone shares their weekly highs and lows can foster open communication and strengthen family ties.

Another crucial step is creating a positive and open communication culture. Encourage family members to discuss their feelings and experiences without fear of criticism. Use active listening to show that you value their perspectives. This means paying attention when someone speaks, asking questions, and reflecting on what you've heard. Open communication helps build trust and ensures that everyone feels heard and understood.

Balancing structure and flexibility in the home is essential for maintaining a nurturing environment. While routines provide a sense of order and predictability, leaving room for spontaneity and adaptability is important. Set routines that include necessary activities like homework and chores and allow for unplanned fun and relaxation. Being adaptable to changes, such as a spontaneous family outing or an impromptu dance party in the living room, can make home life more enjoyable and less rigid.

Consider the story of the Johnson family, who hold regular family meetings every Sunday evening. During these meetings, each family member can speak about their week, voice any concerns, and suggest activities for the upcoming week. This practice keeps everyone informed and makes everyone feel valued and involved in family decisions. Another example is the Smith household, which focuses on emotional well-being. They've created a "calm corner" in their home, filled with comfy cushions, books, and calming activities like coloring and puzzles. Anyone overwhelmed can retreat to this corner to relax and regain their composure.

These real-life examples illustrate that a nurturing home environment is built on emotional safety, support, and open communication. Establishing family rituals and balancing structure with flexibility can transform your home into a sanctuary where every member feels cherished and understood.

Handling Parenting Stress

Parenting is a beautiful yet challenging role that often feels like a constant juggling act. On any given day, you might find yourself balancing work deadlines with school pickups, meal planning with homework help, and still trying to carve out a moment. The stress from juggling these multiple roles can be overwhelming. Society's high expectations only add to the pressure, making you feel like you must excel at everything. This constant strain can lead to burnout, affecting you and your entire family.

To manage this stress, it's crucial to practice self-care and mindfulness. Self-care isn't selfish; it's essential. Take time each day, even if it's just a few minutes, to do something that rejuvenates you. Whether reading a book, taking a walk, or simply sitting quietly with a cup of tea, these moments can help recharge your mental and emotional batteries. Mindfulness practices, such as deep breathing exercises or short meditation sessions, can also be incredibly effective. They help ground you in the present moment, reducing anxiety and helping you approach challenges with a clearer mind.

Seeking support from friends and family can make a world of difference. Don't hesitate to lean on your support network. Share your struggles with a trusted friend or family member; discussing your stress can sometimes alleviate some of the burden. If your stress levels are unmanageable, consider joining a parenting support group. These groups offer a safe space to share experiences and gain insights from others in similar situations. Sometimes, just knowing you're not alone can provide immense relief.

Open communication is another vital aspect of managing parenting stress. Talk to your partner about your stressors and work together to find solutions. Both of you must be on the same page and support each other. Recognize the signs of burnout, such as constant fatigue, irritability, or a sense of detachment, and take action before it worsens. Seek professional help if needed, whether it's through counseling or stress management workshops. Addressing these issues early can prevent them from escalating into more serious problems.

Consider the story of Rebecca, a mother of two who felt overwhelmed by her daily responsibilities. She started practicing mindfulness techniques, such as deep breathing and short meditation, in the mornings before the kids woke up. This simple practice helped her start the day with a sense of calm and focus. Another example is Maria, who joined a local parenting group after feeling isolated and stressed. The support and camaraderie she found there significantly improved her ability to manage stress and find joy in parenting again.

Incorporating these stress-management techniques can transform your daily life. By taking care of yourself, seeking support, and communicating openly, you can handle parenting challenges more effectively and create a healthier, happier environment for your family.

Building Trust with Your Children

Building trust with your children is the cornerstone of a healthy parent-child relationship. Trust forms the foundation for open communication, making it easier for them to come to you with their concerns, joys, and questions. When your child trusts you, they feel secure and confident, knowing they have a safe space to express themselves without fear of judgment. This sense of security is crucial for their emotional development and overall well-being.

Consistency and reliability are key to fostering trust. Children need to know they can count on you to be there when you say you will be. This means following through on promises and being dependable. If you promise to attend their soccer game or help with homework, ensure you do. Consistency in your actions builds a solid foundation of trust over time.

Showing empathy and understanding is another powerful way to build trust. When your child shares their feelings or experiences, listen actively and validate their emotions. Avoid dismissing their concerns, no matter how minor they may seem. Instead, acknowledge their feelings and show that you understand. Phrases like, "I can see that you're upset about this," or "It sounds like that was tough for you," can go a long way in making your child feel heard and understood.

Maintaining trust requires ongoing effort and attention. Keep your promises, no matter how small they may seem. Follow through if you promise a trip to the park on the weekend. Breaking promises can erode trust and make your child reluctant to rely on you in the future. Being present and attentive is equally important. Put away distractions, like your phone or work, and give your child full attention when needed. This shows them that they are your priority and that you value your time together.

Consider the story of Jenna, who promised her daughter a special outing to the zoo on Saturday. Despite a busy week, Jenna kept her promise, and the two had a wonderful day. Following through on a commitment strengthened their bond and reinforced Jenna's reliability in her daughter's eyes. Another example is the Goldstein family, who engage in trust-building games and activities. Every Friday, they have a family game night where everyone gets to choose a game. These activities not only build trust but also foster a sense of teamwork and fun.

Building trust with your children is an ongoing process that requires consistency, empathy, and presence. You can create a strong, trusting relationship that provides a solid foundation for your child's growth and development by being reliable, showing understanding, and maintaining your commitments.

In the next chapter, we'll explore how to navigate societal and cultural pressures, helping you and your family find a path that's true to yourselves amidst external expectations.

Navigating Societal and Cultural Pressures

See yourself at a family gathering, and the conversation turns to your career and personal life. Relatives offer unsolicited advice, subtly hinting that you should focus more on family or implying that your career ambitions are too lofty. You smile politely, but inside, it's a struggle. The pressure to conform to traditional roles is palpable, a challenge many women face daily.

Breaking Free from Traditional Roles

Societal and cultural expectations have long shaped traditional gender roles, influencing how women perceive their roles in both personal and professional spheres. Historically, gender roles have been deeply ingrained, guiding how men and women should behave, think, and interact. Women were often expected to prioritize family and caregiving over personal ambitions. These roles were passed down through generations, creating a framework many still feel compelled to follow. The pressure to conform to these norms can be overwhelming, leading to a constant struggle between fulfilling societal expectations and pursuing personal desires.

These traditional roles often limit personal growth and fulfillment. Internalized expectations can stifle your ambitions and passions, making you feel that certain paths are off-limits. For instance, you might shy away from pursuing a demanding career because it doesn't align with the traditional primary caregiver role. This internal conflict can create a sense of dissatisfaction and unfulfillment as you suppress your true aspirations to fit into a predefined mold. The effect on career choices and personal aspirations can be significant, leading to missed opportunities and unrealized potential.

Breaking free from these traditional roles involves challenging the status quo and setting personal goals independent of societal expectations. Start by reflecting on what you truly want without the influence of external pressures. Write down your goals and aspirations, focusing on what brings you joy and fulfillment. Seek support from like-minded communities where you can share experiences and find encouragement. Surrounding yourself with individuals who understand and support your journey can be empowering and validating.

Consider the story of Mia, who pursued a non-traditional career in engineering. Growing up, she faced constant pressure to choose a more "suitable" profession for women, like teaching or nursing. Despite this, Mia followed her passion for technology and engineering. She faced numerous challenges, including skepticism from family and peers. However, her determination and support from a network of like-minded women in STEM helped her succeed. Today, Mia is a successful engineer, breaking barriers and inspiring other women to pursue their passions.

Another example is Megan, a mother who found a way to balance her career and family life without guilt. Megan felt immense pressure to either focus solely on her career or be a stay-at-home mom. She created her path, setting boundaries and prioritizing tasks aligned with her values. Megan sought flexible work arrangements and involved her family in household responsibilities. This approach allowed her to thrive professionally and personally, showing that balancing multiple roles is possible without succumbing to societal pressures.

Breaking free from traditional roles requires courage and determination, but the rewards are immense. You can create a fulfilling life that aligns with your true self by setting personal goals, seeking support, and challenging societal norms.

Finding Your Path

Imagine sitting at a cozy café, sipping your favorite drink, and daydreaming about what truly excites you. This moment of self-discovery is where finding your path begins. It's about peeling back the layers of societal expectations and focusing on what genuinely ignites your passion. Exploring personal interests and passions is crucial. Think about activities that make you lose track of time. Whether painting, coding, gardening, or writing, these interests often hold the key to your true path. Assessing your strengths and values can further guide you. Reflect on what you're naturally good at and what principles you hold dear. These insights can help shape a life that feels true to you.

Setting personal goals aligned with your values is the next step. This isn't just about career aspirations but about creating a life that resonates with your inner self. Start by creating a vision board. Gather images, quotes, and symbols that represent your dreams and goals. Place it somewhere you can see daily as a visual reminder of what you're working towards. Writing a personal mission statement can also be empowering. This statement should encapsulate what you stand for and aim to achieve. It is a guiding star, helping you stay focused on your path even when obstacles arise.

Obstacles are inevitable, but overcoming them is part of the journey. Dealing with self-doubt and fear is a common challenge. When those negative thoughts creep in, remind yourself of your strengths and achievements. Building resilience and perseverance is essential. Consider setbacks as learning opportunities rather than failures. Surround yourself with supportive people who encourage you to keep going, even when the going gets tough.

Take the story of Sidney, a corporate lawyer who realized her true passion lay in the culinary arts. Despite the stability and prestige of her legal career, she felt unfulfilled. Sidney took a leap of faith, enrolled in culinary school, and eventually opened her own restaurant. Her journey was fraught with challenges, including peer skepticism and financial hurdles. However, her unwavering passion and resilience led her to success, and she now enjoys a fulfilling career that aligns with her true self.

Another inspiring example is Lily, who always dreamed of traveling the world and writing about her experiences. Stuck in a monotonous 9-to-5 job, she felt her dreams slipping away. Determined to change her life, Lily started a travel blog on weekends. It gained traction, and she eventually transitioned to full-time travel writing. Despite societal pressures to maintain a "stable" job, Lily followed her passion and created a life that brought her joy and fulfillment.

Finding your path is about embracing what makes you unique and pursuing it with tenacity. By focusing on self-discovery, setting aligned goals, and overcoming obstacles, you can create a life that reflects your identity.

Handling Societal Expectations

Societal expectations can feel like an invisible weight pressing down on you, dictating how you should act, look, and even think. These expectations often set an impossibly high bar, especially for women.

You're expected to excel in every role you play—whether it's as a mother, employee, partner, or friend. This constant pressure to be perfect can lead to stress and control behaviors. You might be micromanaging every detail of your life, believing it's the only way to meet these high standards. Media and cultural influences play a significant role in shaping these expectations. From glossy magazine covers showcasing flawless mothers to social media feeds filled with curated perfection, it's easy to feel you're falling short. These images and narratives reinforce the idea that you must always have it together.

Setting personal boundaries is crucial to manage these expectations without succumbing to them. This means learning to say no when demands become overwhelming and prioritizing tasks that align with your values. For instance, if you're asked to take on additional work at your job but it interferes with your family time, it's okay to decline. Prioritizing self-care and mental health is also essential. Make time for activities that rejuvenate you, whether reading a book, walking, or practicing yoga. These moments of self-care can help you recharge and maintain your emotional well-being.

Critical thinking is another powerful tool in navigating societal expectations. It's about questioning cultural narratives and making choices based on values rather than societal norms. Ask yourself why you feel compelled to meet certain expectations. Are they aligned with your values, or do external pressures impose them? Making informed choices means being true to yourself and not just following the crowd. This critical evaluation helps you break free from the cycle of control and anxiety that societal expectations can create.

Consider the story of Shari, a mother who rejected the "supermom" stereotype. She felt immense pressure to excel at work, maintain a spotless home, and be constantly available for her children. This unrealistic standard left her exhausted and stressed. Shari decided to set boundaries and prioritize her well-being. She involved her family in household chores, set realistic expectations at work, and made time for self-care. This shift allowed her to find balance and reduce the need for control.

Another example is Kate, a professional who learned to set boundaries to maintain a work-life balance. She faced constant pressure to be available 24/7, leading to burnout. Kate began to set clear boundaries with her employer and colleagues, specifying her work hours and unplugging after office hours. This change improved her mental health and made her more productive and focused during work hours. You can navigate these pressures by managing societal expectations through boundaries, self-care, and critical thinking without losing yourself.

Embracing Your Authentic Self

Authenticity is about being true to yourself and embracing yourself without pretense or fear of judgment. It's about aligning your actions and words with your true beliefs and values. Living authentically means not hiding behind societal masks or trying to fit into boxes that don't suit you. Instead, you're confidently showing up as yourself, with all your unique quirks and traits. Authenticity allows you to live a genuine and fulfilling life, free from the constraints of trying to be something you're not.

Characteristics of authenticity include self-awareness, honesty, and vulnerability. Self-awareness involves understanding your strengths, weaknesses, and true desires. Honesty means being truthful with yourself and others, even when uncomfortable. Vulnerability, though often seen as a weakness, is a strength. It involves embracing your imperfections and being open about your struggles. These traits form the foundation of an authentic life, allowing you to connect deeply with yourself and others.

Living authentically brings numerous benefits. It leads to greater self-confidence because you are no longer trying to be someone you're not. You also experience deeper and more meaningful relationships, as authenticity fosters trust and mutual respect. Additionally, being true to yourself reduces stress and anxiety. You're not constantly worrying about meeting others' expectations or maintaining a facade. Instead, you can relax and enjoy life, knowing that you are living in alignment with your true self.

Embracing your authentic self requires self-acceptance. Start by practicing self-compassion. Treat yourself with the same kindness and understanding that you would offer a friend. When you make mistakes, acknowledge them without harsh self-criticism. Understand that everyone has flaws and that these imperfections make you human. Embracing your vulnerabilities means acknowledging your fears and struggles without shame. It's about understanding that vulnerability is a powerful tool for connection and growth.

Authenticity is crucial in relationships. Communicate openly and honestly with your partner, friends, and family. Share your thoughts, feelings, and desires without fear of judgment. Building connections based on mutual respect means valuing each other's authenticity. Encourage your loved ones to be themselves and appreciate them for who they are. This creates a supportive and nurturing environment where everyone feels valued and understood.

Consider the story of Maria, who embraced her unique identity in her career. She always felt pressured to conform to corporate expectations, hiding her creative side. One day, she incorporated her passion for art into her work. She started leading creative workshops at her company, which brought her joy and improved team dynamics. Her authenticity inspired others to embrace their passions, creating a more innovative and fulfilling workplace.

Another example is Jessica, a mother who fostered authenticity in her family. She encouraged open communication and allowed her children to express their true selves, creating a home environment where everyone felt safe and valued. Jessica's authenticity in her parenting fostered trust and deep connections with her children, creating a supportive and loving family dynamic.

Stories of Women Who Overcame Control Issues

Inspiration often comes from real-life stories, and many women have successfully navigated the challenges of control issues to find balance and fulfillment. Take, for instance, Claire, a high-powered executive in a tech company. Claire spent countless hours micromanaging her team, believing that her meticulous oversight was the only way to succeed. The result? Burnout and strained relationships at work and home. Claire decided enough was enough. She began practicing mindfulness, dedicating a few minutes each morning to meditation. This simple practice helped her stay present and reduce anxiety. Claire also sought therapy, where she learned to trust her team and delegate tasks effectively. Over time, she discovered that letting go of control improved her mental health and boosted her team's productivity and creativity.

Then there's Tenisha, a mother of three who struggled with the pressure to be the perfect parent. Tenisha needed to control every aspect of her children's lives, from homework to extracurricular activities. This constant oversight led to tension and resistance from her kids, who felt stifled. Tenisha realized that her need for control was rooted in anxiety and perfectionism. She started attending a local support group for parents, where she found comfort and practical advice from others facing similar struggles. Tenisha learned to foster independence in her children by giving them more responsibilities and trusting them to make their own decisions. The change was remarkable—her children flourished, becoming more self-reliant and confident, while Tenisha felt a weight lifted off her shoulders.

Another inspiring story is that of Melissa, who balanced a demanding career in finance with her role as a single mother. Melissa's perfectionism drove her to control every detail at work and home, leading to relentless stress. She felt societal and cultural pressures to excel in both arenas, which only heightened her anxiety. Melissa decided to take control of her well-being. She started with self-reflection, journaling her thoughts and feelings to understand her triggers. Through this process, she identified that her fear of failure was a significant driver of her control behaviors. Melissa joined a mindfulness course and began practicing yoga, which helped her find inner peace. She also set realistic goals and boundaries, allowing herself to accept that it's okay not to be perfect. Her newfound balance improved her relationships with colleagues and her child, and she found joy in the present moment.

These stories offer valuable insights and strategies to apply to your life. Persistence and resilience are crucial. Change doesn't happen overnight, but small, consistent steps can lead to significant improvements. Self-compassion is equally important. Be kind to yourself, acknowledging that it's okay to have flaws and make mistakes. Accepting yourself as you are is a powerful step towards reducing control behaviors and finding balance. Seeking support from therapy or community groups can provide the encouragement and tools needed to navigate this journey. Remember, you are not alone, and these stories are a testament to the possibility of transformation.

Strategies for Long-Term Change

Sustainable, long-term change is crucial for truly reducing control behaviors. Short-term fixes might provide temporary relief, but lasting change is what brings about real transformation. Long-term change benefits your mental health and relationships by creating a stable foundation. You'll notice reduced anxiety and stress, more balanced interactions, and overall well-being. Relationships flourish when you're not constantly trying to manage every detail. However, maintaining change over time poses challenges. It's easy to fall back into old habits, especially when life gets stressful. Consistency and patience are your allies in this journey.

To create and maintain long-term change, set realistic and achievable goals. Break down your larger objectives into smaller, manageable steps. For instance, if you want to delegate more at work, begin with a single task. Gradually expand as you become more comfortable. Monitoring your progress is equally important. Keep a journal or use an app to track your achievements and setbacks. This helps you see patterns and adjust strategies as needed. For example, if you notice that you tend to micromanage when stressed, you can implement stress-reduction techniques during those times.

Consistency is key to achieving long-term change. Building habits through repetition helps solidify new behaviors. New habits take time to become second nature, so be patient with yourself. Celebrate small wins along the way. Whether it's a successful week of delegating or a day where you managed to stay calm despite the chaos, acknowledge these victories. They build momentum and reinforce positive change.

Consider the story of Anna, a marketing executive who struggled with work-life balance. She set realistic goals to leave the office by 6 PM at least three days a week. Anna tracked her progress in a journal and made adjustments when she noticed patterns of late nights. Over time, she successfully maintained a healthier work-life balance, feeling more present both at work and home. Her relationships improved as she was less stressed and more engaged with her family.

Another example is Donna, a mother who aimed to create a supportive home environment. She introduced small changes, like weekly family meetings, to discuss everyone's needs and feelings. Donna consistently applied these changes, monitoring their impact on family dynamics. Celebrating small wins, like her children opening up more during these meetings, motivated her to keep going. Over time, these practices became ingrained in their family routine, fostering a more supportive and understanding home environment.

Consistency and patience are essential. It's about making gradual changes that stick. By setting realistic goals, monitoring progress, and celebrating small victories, you can achieve long-term change that significantly reduces control behaviors and enhances your quality of life.

In the next chapter, we'll explore how to build a support network to enhance your well-being further.

TEN

Building a Support Network

Picture yourself sitting in a cozy coffee shop, sipping your latte, and suddenly, you feel the world's weight lifting off your shoulders. Across the table, your best friend listens intently, offering comfort and wisdom. In these moments, you realize the profound impact a strong support network can have on your mental well-being. No one can navigate life's challenges alone, and having a reliable support system can make all the difference.

Importance of a Support Network

A strong support network is like a safety net, catching you when you stumble and lifting you when you're down. The value of having a close-knit circle of friends, family, and professional support cannot be overstated, especially when managing control behaviors and maintaining mental health. Friends provide a listening ear and a different perspective, helping you see situations from angles you may not have considered. They can offer advice grounded in their own experiences, making you feel less isolated in your struggles.

On the other hand, family often provides a sense of unconditional love and acceptance. They know your history, your quirks, and the reasons behind some of your control behaviors. This deep understanding can be comforting, as family members can offer support uniquely tailored to your needs. They can help with practical tasks, provide a shoulder to cry on, or simply be there for a quiet evening at home. However, it's essential to communicate openly with family members about your needs and boundaries to ensure that their support is effective and doesn't inadvertently contribute to your control tendencies.

Professional support, including therapists, counselors, and coaches, is crucial in managing control behaviors. These professionals offer a safe space to explore the root causes of your need for control and develop strategies to address them. Therapists can help you work through past traumas and cognitive distortions that fuel your control issues using evidence-based techniques like Cognitive-Behavioral Therapy (CBT). Coaches, meanwhile, can assist you in setting realistic goals and developing actionable plans to achieve them, providing accountability and motivation along the way.

It's important to recognize that different types of support serve different purposes. Friends and family offer emotional and practical support, while professionals provide specialized guidance and therapeutic interventions. Each type of support complements the others, creating a comprehensive network that addresses various aspects of your well-being.

Having a diverse support network also means you're not overly reliant on one person or type of support. This diversity can prevent burnout and ensure you have multiple sources of strength to draw. For example, while a friend might be great for a late-night chat, a therapist can offer structured interventions to tackle deep-seated issues. Similarly, family members might provide practical help with daily tasks, freeing up your mental space to focus on personal growth and self-care.

It's also worth noting that building and maintaining a support network requires effort and reciprocity. Investing time and energy into your relationships and showing up for others as you'd like them to show up for you is essential. This reciprocity fosters trust and deepens connections, making your support network even more robust. Consider contacting friends regularly, checking in with family members, and attending therapy sessions consistently. These small acts of connection can significantly impact your overall well-being.

Reflecting on your current support network, you might find areas where it could be strengthened. Are there friends you've lost touch with who you could reconnect with? Are there family members you could communicate more openly with? Is there a professional you've been considering seeing but haven't yet taken the step to contact? Taking proactive steps to build and nurture your support network can enhance your ability to manage control behaviors and improve your mental health.

Reflection Exercise: Assessing Your Support Network

Take a moment to reflect on your current support network. Consider the following questions and jot down your thoughts in a journal:

1. Who are the key people in your support network (friends, family, professionals)?
2. How often do you reach out to them for support?
3. Are there areas where your support network could be strengthened?
4. What steps can you take to build or enhance your support network?

By thoughtfully assessing your support network and taking proactive steps to strengthen it, you can create a more resilient foundation for managing control behaviors and maintaining mental health. Remember, you're not alone in this journey; having a strong support network can make all the difference.

Finding and Cultivating Support

Building a support network can feel daunting, especially if you're already juggling numerous responsibilities. But finding like-minded communities and professional help can be incredibly rewarding. Start by considering your interests and current social circles. Are there people you already know who share similar goals or challenges? Reaching out to friends or acquaintances with whom you feel connected can be a great first step. Let them know you're looking to build a supportive network and see if they want to join it. Opening up to others can sometimes pave the way to deeper, more meaningful connections.

Local community groups are another excellent resource. Libraries, community centers, and local bulletin boards list various clubs and groups. Whether it's a book club, a fitness class, or a hobby group, participating in these activities can help you meet people with shared interests. Don't be afraid to attend a meeting to see if it's a good fit. These settings often provide a relaxed atmosphere where you can gradually build relationships without the pressure to open up about personal struggles immediately.

Online communities have become an invaluable support resource for those with busy schedules or limited local options. Websites like Meetup.com offer virtual groups tailored to various interests and needs. From parenting forums to professional development networks, there's likely an online community that aligns with your interests. Social media platforms can also be useful if navigated mindfully. For instance, Facebook groups host various supportive communities where members share advice, experiences, and encouragement. Just ensure you choose positive and constructive groups, avoiding those that might contribute to stress or negativity.

Support groups, both online and offline, provide a structured environment for sharing and listening. Professionals or experienced volunteers often facilitate these groups, ensuring that discussions remain focused and supportive. Look for groups that address specific issues you're dealing with, such as anxiety, parenting, or work-life balance. Participating in a support group can help you realize that you're not alone in your struggles, and hearing others' experiences can offer new perspectives and coping strategies.

Therapy is another cornerstone of a strong support network. A good therapist can offer personalized guidance and help you navigate complex emotions and behaviors. If you're new to therapy, consider asking friends or your primary care doctor for recommendations. Many therapists offer initial consultations, allowing you to find someone you feel comfortable with. Don't be discouraged if it takes a few tries to find the right fit—trust and rapport are crucial for effective therapy.

Coaching can also be incredibly beneficial, especially if you want to achieve specific goals or make significant changes in your life. Life, career, and wellness coaches can provide targeted support and accountability. They can help you break down your goals into manageable steps and offer strategies to overcome obstacles. While coaching is often more action-oriented than therapy, it can complement therapeutic work by providing practical tools and motivation.

If you're a parent, finding and cultivating support can be challenging and incredibly rewarding. Parenting groups, whether in-person or virtual, can offer a sense of camaraderie and shared experience. These groups provide a space to share tips, vent frustrations, and celebrate victories. Look for groups that align with your parenting style and values, ensuring that the advice and support you receive are relevant and helpful.

For professional women, networking groups and associations can be invaluable. Organizations like Lean In Circles, professional guilds, and industry-specific groups offer both support and opportunities for growth. These groups often host events, webinars, and forums where you can connect with peers, mentors, and potential collaborators. Building relationships in these settings can provide emotional support, professional opportunities, and resources.

When cultivating your support network, being proactive and intentional is essential. Regularly contact your contacts, schedule meetups or calls, and participate actively in group activities. Show genuine interest in others' lives and offer support in return. Building a support network is a reciprocal process, and the effort you put in will often be reflected in the support you receive.

Maintaining Healthy Relationships

Imagine you're catching up with a close friend over lunch, and as you both share updates about your lives, you realize how much you rely on each other for support. This kind of relationship doesn't happen overnight; it requires effort, care, and reciprocity. Nurturing and maintaining healthy relationships within your support network is crucial for lasting emotional well-being and mutual growth.

One of the most important aspects of maintaining healthy relationships is the concept of reciprocity. It's not just about what you can get from the relationship but also what you can give. Mutual support is the foundation of any strong relationship. When your friend is going through a tough time, offer a listening ear or a helping hand. Likewise, don't hesitate to lean on them when you need support. This balance of give and take creates a sense of trust and reliability, making both parties feel valued and understood.

Communication is another cornerstone of healthy relationships. It's essential to be open and honest about your needs and boundaries. If you're feeling overwhelmed, let your friend or family member know. They can't read your mind, and clear communication helps avoid misunderstandings. On the flip side, make an effort to listen actively when they share their thoughts and feelings. Active listening means being fully present in the conversation, showing empathy, and reflecting on what you've heard to ensure understanding. This practice strengthens your bond and makes the other person feel heard and valued.

Consistency is key to maintaining healthy relationships. Regular check-ins, whether through text, phone calls, or in-person meetups, help keep the connection strong. It shows that you care and are invested in the relationship. Even a quick message to ask how someone's day is going can make a significant difference. Consistency also means being reliable—following through on promises and being there when you say you will. This reliability builds trust, which is the bedrock of any healthy relationship.

It's also important to practice empathy and understanding. Everyone has their struggles and challenges, and sometimes, your friends or family members might not be able to offer support in the way you need. Instead of feeling hurt or frustrated, try to understand their perspective. Empathy allows you to see things from their point of view, which can deepen your connection and foster a more supportive relationship. Remember, it's not always about having the right words; sometimes, just being there is enough.

Boundaries are crucial in any relationship. They ensure that both parties feel respected and valued. Be clear about your boundaries and respect those of others. If you need alone time to recharge, communicate that openly. Likewise, if a friend sets a boundary, honor it without taking it personally. Boundaries help maintain a healthy balance and prevent feelings of resentment or burnout.

Building rituals can also help maintain healthy relationships. These can be as simple as a weekly coffee date, a monthly book club, or a yearly getaway. Rituals create shared experiences that strengthen your bond and provide something to look forward to. They offer a sense of stability and continuity, which can be comforting amidst life's uncertainties.

Conflict is inevitable in any relationship, but how you handle it can make all the difference. Approach conflicts with a mindset of resolution rather than blame. Use "I" statements to express your feelings without accusing others. For example, say, "I feel hurt when you don't respond to my messages," rather than, "You never respond to me." This approach fosters open dialogue and helps resolve issues without damaging the relationship.

Lastly, celebrate each other's successes and milestones. Whether it's a job promotion, a personal achievement, or a small victory, acknowledging and celebrating these moments shows that you care about their happiness and well-being. It adds a positive dimension to your relationship and creates joyful memories.

Maintaining healthy relationships within your support network requires effort, but the rewards are immense. These relationships provide a sense of belonging, reduce stress, and enhance overall quality of life. By focusing on reciprocity, communication, consistency, empathy, boundaries, rituals, conflict resolution, and celebration, you can nurture relationships that are not only supportive but also deeply fulfilling.

Success Stories

Consider Sarah, a high-achieving marketing executive who always felt like she was carrying the world's weight on her shoulders. Her need to control every aspect of her work and home life left her exhausted and isolated. One day, Sarah decided she couldn't continue like this. She started small by reaching out to a colleague she trusted and respected. Over coffee, she opened up about her struggles with control and anxiety. To her surprise, her colleague shared similar experiences. They began to meet regularly, forming a mini-support network within their office. This simple act of sharing not only eased Sarah's stress but also fostered a sense of camaraderie and mutual support. As Sarah's network grew, she became more willing to delegate tasks and trust her team, leading to increased productivity and a healthier work-life balance.

Then there's Shelly, a single mom navigating the challenges of raising two teenagers while managing a demanding career. Shelly always felt like she had to do it all—be the perfect mom, the ideal employee, and still find time for herself. The constant juggling act took a toll on her mental health, and she knew she needed help. Shelly joined an online parenting group where she found other single moms facing similar challenges. The group became a lifeline, offering practical advice, emotional support, and a safe space to vent. This network taught Shelly to set realistic expectations for herself and her kids. She realized that asking for help wasn't a sign of weakness but a strength. Her support network helped her manage her stress and enriched her parenting experience, making her feel more connected and less alone.

Emma's story highlights the importance of professional support. Emma was a successful lawyer who struggled with perfectionism and control issues. The pressure to be flawless in her career was overwhelming. She decided to seek therapy to understand the root causes of her behavior. Her therapist helped her uncover deep-seated fears of failure and inadequacy that drove her need for control. Through therapy, Emma learned coping strategies to manage her anxiety and perfectionism. Additionally, she joined a professional women's network where she met mentors who provided guidance and support. This combination of professional help and peer support allowed Emma to find balance in her life, reducing her stress and improving her performance at work.

Emma's experience underscores the power of community. As a new mom, Emma felt isolated and overwhelmed by the demands of caring for her newborn. She joined a local mom's group, hoping to find support and advice. What she found was so much more. The group offered a space where she could share her fears, frustrations, and joys without judgment. She formed close friendships with other moms who understood exactly what she was going through. These women became her support network, offering practical help like babysitting swaps and moral support during those sleepless nights. With their help, Emma learned to let go of her need for control and embrace the messiness of motherhood. Her mental health improved, and she felt more confident and capable as a parent.

Consider Charlotte's journey as a professional woman striving to balance her career and personal life. Charlotte was always in control at work, but this often left her feeling drained and disconnected from her loved ones. She joined a professional women's group focused on work-life balance. Through this group, Charlotte met women who were facing similar challenges. They shared strategies for setting boundaries, delegating tasks, and prioritizing self-care. This support network became a source of inspiration and motivation for Charlotte. She learned to set realistic goals for herself, both professionally and personally. Her newfound balance improved her mental health and enhanced her relationships with her family and colleagues.

These success stories illustrate the transformative power of a strong support network. Whether it's friends, family, professional help, or community groups, having a network of supportive individuals can make a significant difference in managing control behaviors and maintaining mental health. As you reflect on these stories, consider the steps you can take to build and nurture your support network.

Remember, you're not alone; seeking support is a courageous and empowering choice.

In the next chapter, we'll explore the importance of embracing flexibility and adaptability in various aspects of life and provide practical tools to help you gracefully navigate unexpected changes and challenges.

Embracing Flexibility and Adaptability

Imagine you're at a company meeting, the kind that usually makes you tense. The agenda is packed, your to-do list is overflowing, and you've meticulously planned your day to the minute. Suddenly, your boss announces a major shift in the project's direction. Your heart races, your palms sweat, and you feel panicked. What now? This scenario is all too familiar for many of us who crave control. The unexpected throws us off balance, leaving us scrambling to regain a sense of order. But what if I told you that embracing flexibility could help you navigate these changes gracefully, reduce stress, and improve your relationships?

Understanding Flexibility

Flexibility and adaptability are more than just buzzwords; they are essential life skills that can significantly enhance your well-being and effectiveness. Flexibility means adjusting your thoughts, behaviors, and plans in response to new information or changing circumstances. It's about letting go of rigid expectations and finding alternative ways to achieve your goals. Adaptability, on the other hand, is the capacity to thrive in different environments and situations. It involves a willingness to learn, unlearn, and relearn, as well as the ability to cope with uncertainty and change.

In practical terms, flexibility is like adjusting your work schedule to accommodate a sudden family obligation or changing your approach to a project when new challenges arise. Adaptability could involve learning new skills to stay relevant in a rapidly evolving job market or finding joy in unplanned moments of spontaneity. Both qualities require a mindset shift from a fixed to a growth-oriented perspective, where setbacks are seen as opportunities for learning and growth rather than failures.

The benefits of flexibility are manifold. For one, it significantly reduces control tendencies. When you're flexible, you're less likely to feel the need to micromanage every detail of your life. Instead, you can trust that things will work out, even if they don't go as planned. This trust can lead to a profound reduction in anxiety and stress. You'll find yourself more resilient and better able to handle life's ups and downs without feeling overwhelmed.

Flexibility also enhances your relationships. When you're adaptable, you're more open to others' ideas and perspectives. This openness fosters better communication and collaboration, whether at home or work. For instance, if your partner suggests a last-minute change in weekend plans, your ability to adapt can turn a potential conflict into an opportunity for a new adventure. In the workplace, being flexible can make you a more valuable team member, as you'll be better equipped to handle changes in project scope or deadlines with a positive attitude.

Moreover, being flexible can improve your overall well-being. Studies have shown that individuals who exhibit higher levels of flexibility tend to experience greater life satisfaction and emotional stability.

This is because flexibility allows you to navigate life's challenges more effectively, reducing the emotional toll of unexpected events. You become more adept at managing stress, leading to better physical health. Adaptability can also enhance your problem-solving skills, as you'll be more willing to explore different solutions than a single, rigid approach.

Flexibility and adaptability are not innate traits but skills that can be developed with practice. Start by embracing small changes in your daily routine. For example, take a different route to work or try a new hobby. These seemingly minor adjustments can help you become more comfortable with change and uncertainty. Gradually, you can tackle larger shifts, such as taking on a new role at work or moving to a new city. The key is approaching these changes with an open mind and a willingness to learn.

One way to cultivate flexibility is through mindfulness practices. Mindfulness helps you stay present in the moment, reducing the tendency to overthink and stress about the future. When you're mindful, you can approach change with curiosity rather than fear. Mindfulness techniques, such as deep breathing or meditation, can also help you stay calm and focused during turbulent times, making it easier to adapt to new circumstances.

Another effective strategy is to reframe your mindset. Instead of viewing change as a threat, see it as an opportunity for growth. This shift in perspective can significantly change how you respond to new situations. For instance, if a project at work suddenly takes a different direction, view it as a chance to develop new skills or showcase your creativity. This positive outlook can reduce the stress associated with change and make you more resilient.

Building a support network is also crucial for developing flexibility. Surround yourself with people who encourage and support your growth. Whether it's friends, family, or colleagues, having a strong support system can provide the emotional resilience needed to navigate change. They can offer different perspectives and practical advice, making it easier to adapt to new situations.

Remember, flexibility is a journey, not a destination. It's about progress, not perfection. The more you practice, the more natural it will become. Over time, you'll find that flexibility helps you manage control tendencies and enriches your life in ways you never imagined. So, the next time you face an unexpected change, take a deep breath, embrace the uncertainty, and remember that flexibility is your ally in this ever-changing world.

Reflection Exercise: Embracing Flexibility

Take a few moments to reflect on recent changes or challenges in your life. How did you respond to them? Were there opportunities where you could have been more flexible? Name three specific instances where embracing flexibility could have made a positive difference. Consider how you can approach similar situations in the future with a more adaptable mindset. Reflecting on these experiences can help you identify areas for growth and reinforce the importance of flexibility in your daily life.

Developing Adaptability Skills

You're in a busy workday, your schedule packed with meetings and deadlines. Suddenly, your boss drops a new, urgent project on your desk. Your initial reaction is to panic. But instead of letting that stress take over, imagine being able to adapt seamlessly to this change, shifting your priorities without losing your cool. Developing adaptability is key to managing these unexpected challenges without resorting to control. Let's explore some exercises and strategies that can help you become more adaptable in your daily life.

One effective way to develop adaptability is to start small. Begin with minor changes in your routine that don't carry much risk. For example, try switching up your morning routine. If you usually start your day by checking emails, spend the first 30 minutes on a mindfulness exercise or light stretching instead. This small shift can help you become more comfortable with change and break the habit of rigid routines. Over time, these small adaptations can build confidence in handling larger, more significant changes.

Another powerful exercise is to deliberately put yourself in new and unfamiliar situations. This could be as simple as taking a different route to work or trying a new hobby. Exposing yourself to new experiences teaches you to navigate uncertainty and become more comfortable with the unknown. For instance, if you've always been interested in painting but never tried it, sign up for a beginner's class. Learning something new, making mistakes, and improving over time can be incredibly empowering and enhance your ability to adapt to new challenges in other areas of your life.

Practicing mindfulness can also be a game-changer. Mindfulness helps you stay present and focused, reducing the tendency to overthink and stress about future uncertainties. When you practice mindfulness, you learn to observe your thoughts and feelings without judgment, allowing you to respond to changes more calmly and thoughtfully. Try incorporating short mindfulness sessions into your daily routine. Even five minutes of focused breathing or a quick body scan can make a difference. Over time, mindfulness can help you develop a more adaptable mindset, making it easier to go with the flow when unexpected changes arise.

Adopting a growth mindset is another crucial strategy. A growth mindset, instead of a fixed mindset, embraces challenges as opportunities for learning and growth. When you encounter an unexpected change, instead of seeing it as a threat, view it as a chance to develop new skills or gain new insights. For example, if a project at work takes an unexpected turn, see it as an opportunity to showcase your problem-solving skills or learn a new aspect of the business. This shift in perspective can reduce the stress associated with change and make you more resilient.

Building a support network is also essential for developing adaptability. Surround yourself with people who encourage and support your growth. Whether it's friends, family, or colleagues, having a strong support system can provide the emotional resilience needed to navigate change. They can offer different perspectives and practical advice, making it easier to adapt to new situations. For instance, discussing a significant change at work with a trusted colleague can provide valuable insights and help you feel more confident handling it.

To handle unexpected changes without resorting to control, it's important to develop a flexible mindset. This involves being open to new possibilities and adjusting your plans as needed. One way to cultivate this mindset is to practice saying "yes" more often. When opportunities arise, even outside your comfort zone, consider saying yes and seeing where it leads. This doesn't mean you should agree to everything, but being more open to new experiences can help you become more adaptable.

Another strategy is to create contingency plans. While predicting every possible outcome is impossible, having a few backup plans can make it easier to adapt when things don't go as expected. For example, if you're planning a big presentation at work, think about potential obstacles that could arise, such as technical issues or unexpected questions. Having a plan in place for these scenarios can reduce anxiety and help you feel more prepared to handle whatever comes your way.

It's also helpful to practice letting go of the need for perfection. Understand that things won't always go according to plan, and that's okay. Instead of striving for perfection, focus on progress and learning. For instance, if a project doesn't turn out exactly as you envisioned, take a step back and evaluate what you've learned from the experience. This can help you see the value in the process itself rather than just the outcome.

Journaling can be a valuable tool for developing adaptability. Take time each day to reflect on how you handled unexpected changes or challenges. Write down what went well, what didn't, and what you can learn from the experience. This practice can help you identify patterns in your behavior and develop strategies for responding more adaptively in the future.

Lastly, practice gratitude. Focusing on what you're grateful for makes it easier to maintain a positive outlook even when things don't go as planned. Try keeping a gratitude journal where you write down three things you're grateful for daily. This simple practice can shift your mindset from scarcity and control to abundance and adaptability.

Developing adaptability is a continuous process, but with practice, it can become second nature. By incorporating these exercises and strategies into your daily life, you can become more resilient, reduce your need for control, and easily navigate life's unexpected challenges.

Real-Life Application

Meet Val, a marketing executive who used to feel like she had to control every aspect of her job and home life. Val was known for her meticulous planning and ability to juggle multiple tasks. However, this constant need for control started taking a toll on her mental health and her relationships. She felt perpetually stressed and anxious, and her colleagues often felt micromanaged.

Val decided it was time to make a change. She started by incorporating small changes into her daily routine. Instead of sticking to her rigid schedule, she allowed herself some flexibility. If a meeting ran over time, she didn't panic. She simply adjusted her plan for the day. This small shift in mindset made a huge difference. She felt more relaxed and was able to focus better on her tasks.

In her personal life, Val applied the same principles. She started saying "yes" to spontaneous plans with friends and family. Instead of planning every detail of her weekends, she left room for unplanned activities. This made her weekends more enjoyable and less stressful. Val's relationships improved as her friends and family appreciated her newfound spontaneity and openness.

Another inspiring story is Jasmine, a single mother of two who works as a nurse. Jasmine's job is demanding, with long shifts and the occasional emergency call. She used to feel overwhelmed by the unpredictability of her schedule and the demands of parenting. Jasmine decided to embrace flexibility to manage her stress better. She began by creating a more adaptable daily routine. She arranged for a neighbor to pick up her kids from school if she had to stay late at work. She also learned to let go of the need for a spotless home, focusing instead on spending quality time with her children.

Jasmine also practiced mindfulness to stay present and reduce anxiety. She would take a few minutes each morning to meditate and set positive intentions for the day. This practice helped her stay calm and focused, even when her day didn't go as planned. Jasmine's new approach improved her mental health and strengthened her bond with her children. They appreciated her relaxed demeanor and the time they spent together, free from the stress of a rigid schedule.

Then there's Kim, a project manager in a tech company. Kim's role required her to oversee multiple projects simultaneously, each with its challenges and deadlines. She often found herself trying to control every detail, which led to burnout and strained relationships with her team. Kim took a different approach by delegating tasks and trusting her team more. She started by identifying tasks that others could handle and trained her team to take on more responsibilities. This lightened her workload and empowered her team members, making them feel more valued and engaged.

Kim also worked on her adaptability by embracing a growth mindset. She viewed a project as an opportunity to learn and grow whenever it faced unexpected changes. Instead of stressing over deviations from the plan, she focused on finding creative solutions. This positive attitude was contagious, and her team became more resilient and innovative. Kim's flexibility and adaptability improved her work-life balance and made her a more effective leader.

Alison's story is another great example. She is a freelance graphic designer who used to struggle with the unpredictability of freelancing. The feast-or-famine cycle of freelance work often left her feeling anxious and stressed. Alison decided to embrace flexibility by diversifying her client base and income streams. She started offering online workshops and selling digital products in addition to her client work. This provided a more stable income and allowed her to explore new creative avenues.

Alison also practiced flexibility in her daily routine. Instead of sticking to a strict 9-to-5 schedule, she allowed herself to work during her most productive hours, whether early in the morning or late at night. She also made time for self-care activities like yoga and reading, which helped her stay balanced and energized. Alison's adaptable approach to freelancing reduced her stress and made her work more enjoyable and fulfilling.

These real-life stories demonstrate the power of embracing flexibility and adaptability. Whether it's adjusting your daily routine, delegating tasks, or exploring new opportunities, being flexible can significantly reduce stress and improve your overall well-being. It can also enhance your relationships, making you more open to others' ideas and perspectives. By learning to go with the flow, you can navigate life's challenges more easily and confidently.

As we've seen, flexibility is not just about reacting to changes but proactively creating a life that allows adaptation. It's about finding balance and embracing the unexpected moments that make life rich and fulfilling. In the next chapter, we'll explore how to create a personal action plan to apply these principles in your own life.

TWELVE

Creating a Personal Action Plan

See yourself sitting at your favorite café, savoring a cup of coffee, and feeling a bit overwhelmed by the sheer number of things on your to-do list. You've read about mindfulness, deep breathing exercises, and the importance of setting boundaries, but putting it all into practice feels daunting. That's where a personal action plan comes in. It's your roadmap to reducing control behaviors and achieving a balanced, fulfilling life. You can make meaningful progress without feeling overwhelmed by breaking down your goals into manageable steps.

Developing an Action Plan

Creating a personalized action plan starts with understanding your unique needs and challenges. Think of it as crafting a tailored recipe for success that considers your specific ingredients and desired outcomes. Start by identifying the areas where you struggle most with control. Is it at work where you find yourself micromanaging every detail? Or at home, where you feel the need to oversee every aspect of your family's routine? Once you've pinpointed these areas, you can begin setting clear, achievable goals.

Begin by setting SMART goals—Specific, Measurable, Achievable, Relevant, and Time-bound goals. For example, instead of saying, "I want to stop micromanaging at work," you might set a goal like, "I will delegate at least one task to a team member each day for the next month." This goal is specific (delegating tasks), measurable (one task per day), achievable (manageable within your daily routine), relevant (directly addresses micromanaging), and time-bound (over the next month).

Next, break these goals down into smaller, actionable steps. Let's take the goal of delegating tasks at work. The first step might be to identify tasks that can be delegated. Make a list of all your current responsibilities and highlight those that don't require your direct involvement. The next step could be communicating with your team, explaining the importance of delegation and how it will benefit you and them. Finally, you might set a reminder to delegate one task each day, gradually building this new habit.

Tracking your progress as you work on these steps is crucial. Keeping a journal or using a digital tracker can be incredibly helpful. Note each task you delegate and reflect on how it feels to let go of control. Are you experiencing less stress? How is your team responding? Tracking these details will help you see the progress you're making and stay motivated.

In addition to tracking progress, reflection is a key component of your action plan. Set aside time each week to review your journal or tracker. Reflect on what's working well and what challenges you've faced. This reflection period allows you to celebrate your successes and identify areas where you might need to adjust your approach. For example, if you find that delegating tasks has reduced your stress but still feel overwhelmed by your workload, you might need to set additional boundaries or seek further support.

To help you get started, I've included a template for setting goals, tracking progress, and reflecting on achievements. Feel free to customize it to fit your needs.

Personal Action Plan Template

Goal Setting:

1. **Identify Areas of Struggle:**
   - Work: Micromanaging tasks
   - Home: Overseeing family routines
   - Relationships: Controlling conversations
2. **Set SMART Goals:**
   - Work: "I will delegate at least one task to a team member each day for the next month."
   - Home: "I will allow my partner to handle dinner plans twice a week."
   - Relationships: "I will practice active listening without interrupting during conversations."

Actionable Steps:

1. **Break Down Goals:**
   - Delegating Tasks at Work:
     - List all current responsibilities
     - Highlight tasks that can be delegated
     - Communicate with the team about delegation
     - Set daily reminders to delegate one task
2. **Home and Relationships:**
   - Allow Partner to Handle Dinner Plans:
     - Discuss the plan with your partner
     - Schedule which days they'll handle dinner
     - Provide support without taking over
   - Practice Active Listening:

- Set a goal to listen during one conversation each day actively
- Reflect on the experience in your journal

Tracking Progress:

1. **Daily Tracking:**
   - Use a journal or digital tracker to note each task you delegate, each dinner plan handled by your partner, and each time you practice active listening.
   - Record your feelings and observations.
2. **Weekly Reflection:**
   - Review your journal or tracker.
   - Reflect on what's working well and any challenges faced.
   - Adjust your approach as needed.

Reflection Questions:

1. **Successes:**
   - What tasks did I successfully delegate this week?
   - How did it feel to let go of control?
   - What positive changes have I noticed in my stress levels and team dynamics?
2. **Challenges:**
   - What obstacles did I encounter?
   - How can I address these challenges moving forward?
   - Do I need to adjust my goals or steps?
3. **Adjustments:**
   - Are there additional boundaries I need to set?
   - Is there further support I need to seek?
   - How can I continue to build on my successes?

Creating a personal action plan isn't about achieving perfection; it's about making steady progress toward a more balanced and fulfilling life. Be kind to yourself throughout this process. Remember that change takes time and effort, and it's okay to make adjustments along the way. Celebrate your successes, no matter how small, and use any setbacks as learning opportunities.

Having a support system in place is also helpful as you work on your action plan. Share your goals with a trusted friend, family member, or mentor who can offer encouragement and hold you accountable. Having someone to check in with can make a significant difference in staying motivated and committed to your plan.

Incorporate self-care practices into your action plan to support your overall well-being. Mindfulness exercises, deep breathing techniques, and regular physical activity can help manage stress and keep you focused. Make sure to schedule time for these activities, treating them as non-negotiable parts of your routine.

Finally, be patient with yourself. Reducing control behaviors and embracing flexibility is a journey that requires persistence and self-compassion. Celebrate each step forward and acknowledge your effort to create positive change. You're taking important steps toward a more balanced, fulfilling life, and that's something to be proud of.

Setting Milestones and Rewards

Imagine you're climbing a mountain. The peak feels impossibly far away, but there are small plateaus along the way where you can rest, catch your breath, and appreciate how far you've come. This is what setting milestones is like on your path to reducing control behaviors. Milestones are essential because they break down a daunting goal into manageable chunks, making progress feel achievable and less overwhelming.

Milestones act as mini-goals that keep you focused and motivated. For example, if your primary goal is to let go of micromanaging at work, a milestone could be delegating one significant task per week. Another milestone might be to receive positive feedback from a team member about your delegation skills. These smaller goals help you maintain momentum and provide opportunities to celebrate your progress, reinforcing your motivation to continue.

Celebrating these milestones is just as crucial as setting them. Think of it as giving yourself a well-deserved pat on the back. Recognition, whether from yourself or others, can significantly boost your morale and reinforce positive behaviors. It's important to choose rewards that are meaningful to you, and that genuinely feel like a treat. These rewards don't have to be extravagant; they just need to be something that brings you joy and satisfaction.

Incorporating rewards can be as simple as allowing yourself some extra downtime. For instance, after successfully delegating tasks for a week, you might reward yourself with a relaxing evening off, indulging in a favorite hobby, or spending time with loved ones. If you've reached a more significant milestone, such as consistently practicing mindfulness for a month, consider treating yourself to a spa day or a weekend getaway. The key is that the reward should feel like a genuine acknowledgment of your hard work and progress.

Another idea for meaningful rewards is to invest in something that further supports your goals. Suppose you've been working on reducing control behaviors at home by allowing your partner to handle more responsibilities. As a reward, you might invest in a family activity that fosters togetherness and fun, like a game night or a day trip. This not only celebrates your progress but also strengthens the bonds within your family.

You can also consider rewards that promote self-care and well-being. For example, after reaching a milestone, treat yourself to a new book, a yoga class, or a session with a coach or therapist. These rewards not only acknowledge your achievements but also contribute to your ongoing personal growth and mental health.

In addition to personal rewards, sharing your milestones and achievements with others can be incredibly powerful. Tell a close friend, family member, or mentor about your progress. Their encouragement and recognition can further boost your confidence and motivation. You might even consider celebrating together, such as going out for a celebratory meal or engaging in a fun activity that you both enjoy.

It's also helpful to document your milestones and rewards. Keeping a visual record, like a progress chart or a journal, can provide a tangible reminder of how far you've come. Each time you look at this record, you'll see a visual representation of your efforts and successes, which can be incredibly motivating during challenging times.

Creating a milestone and reward checklist can be beneficial for those who thrive on structure. Write down your primary goal, break it into smaller milestones, and next to each milestone, note the reward you'll give yourself upon achieving it. This checklist can serve as a roadmap, guiding you through your journey with clear markers of progress and celebration.

As you continue to reach milestones and celebrate your successes, you'll likely notice a shift in your mindset. The process of setting and achieving small goals can build your confidence and reinforce the belief that you are capable of change. It can also help you develop a more positive and proactive attitude toward your goals, making the overall process feel less daunting.

Remember, the purpose of rewards is not just to mark progress but to make the journey enjoyable and fulfilling. By acknowledging your efforts and celebrating your achievements, you're reinforcing the positive changes you're making in your life. This not only helps you stay motivated but also makes the process of reducing control behaviors a rewarding and enriching experience in itself.

In essence, setting milestones and celebrating progress is about creating a balanced and sustainable approach to personal growth. It's about recognizing that each step you take, no matter how small, is a victory worth celebrating. So, as you continue on your path toward reducing control behaviors, make sure to pause, appreciate your progress, and reward yourself for the incredible effort you're putting in.

Maintaining Motivation

Staying motivated on your personal growth journey can be challenging, especially when life throws curveballs your way. But keeping that spark alive is crucial to making lasting changes. One effective way to stay motivated is to regularly remind yourself why you started this journey in the first place. Visualize the benefits of reducing control behaviors—imagine less stress, more fulfilling relationships, and a greater sense of peace. Write down these benefits and place them somewhere visible, like your bathroom mirror or your workspace. This constant reminder of your "why" can reignite your motivation on tough days.

Another key to maintaining motivation is to surround yourself with positive influences. Engage with a community of like-minded individuals who are also working on personal growth. This could be a local support group, an online forum, or even a few close friends who share similar goals. Sharing your experiences, challenges, and successes with others creates a sense of camaraderie and support. Knowing you're not alone in your journey can make all the difference. Plus, celebrating each other's milestones can be incredibly uplifting and encouraging.

It's also helpful to break your goals into smaller, more manageable tasks. When you see progress in smaller increments, it feels less overwhelming and more achievable. Instead of focusing on the end goal, concentrate on the next step you need to take. For example, if your goal is to delegate more at work, start with one small task. Once you've successfully delegated that task, move on to the next. This approach not only makes the process more manageable but also allows you to celebrate small wins along the way, which boosts your motivation.

Creating a routine can also keep you on track. Incorporate time for self-reflection, mindfulness, or any other practices that help you stay focused and calm. Consistency is key. Even on days when you don't feel like it, sticking to your routine can help maintain momentum. Remember, it's okay to have off days. What matters is getting back on track. A routine provides structure, which can be comforting and motivating, especially when life feels chaotic.

Setbacks are inevitable, but they don't have to derail your progress. When you face a setback, it's important to approach it with a growth mindset. Instead of viewing the setback as a failure, see it as a learning opportunity. Ask yourself what you can learn from the experience and how you can apply that lesson moving forward. This shift in perspective can turn setbacks into valuable stepping stones on your path to growth. Remember, progress isn't always linear, and that's okay.

Another effective strategy is to mix things up. Sometimes, monotony can sap your motivation. If you find yourself in a rut, try changing your approach. This could mean switching up your routine, trying a new mindfulness exercise, or setting a new short-term goal. Variety keeps things interesting and can rekindle your enthusiasm. Experiment with different strategies until you find what works best for you.

Accountability is another powerful motivator. Share your goals with someone you trust and ask them to hold you accountable. Regular check-ins with this person can keep you focused and committed. Knowing that someone else is invested in your progress can provide an extra boost of motivation. Whether it's a friend, family member, or coach, having someone to support and encourage you can make a significant difference.

Lastly, practice self-compassion. Be kind to yourself, especially on tough days. Remember that personal growth is a process, not a destination. It's okay to make mistakes and have setbacks. What's important is that you're making an effort and taking steps toward positive change. Treat yourself with the same kindness and understanding that you would offer a friend. This self-compassion not only boosts your motivation but also fosters a healthier, more positive mindset.

In summary, staying motivated involves a combination of reminding yourself of your why, surrounding yourself with positive influences, breaking goals into manageable tasks, creating a routine, viewing setbacks as learning opportunities, mixing things up, seeking accountability, and practicing self-compassion. These strategies can help you stay committed to your action plan and continue making progress toward your goals. Personal growth is a journey, and maintaining motivation is key to navigating it successfully. As you continue on this path, remember to celebrate your progress, no matter how small, and keep pushing forward.

Conclusion

It's been quite a journey, hasn't it? We've dived deep into understanding what it means to be a control freak and, more importantly, how to release that control. This book opened with recognizing and understanding control behaviors, helping you see how they manifest in daily life and their impact on mental health and relationships. We then moved on to practical tools like mindfulness and deep breathing exercises to help you manage stress and anxiety.

We explored enhancing mental health with techniques like Cognitive-Behavioral Therapy (CBT), stress-reduction methods, and the importance of sleep, nutrition, and exercise. We also delved into the power of self-reflection, using journaling and reflective questions to uncover hidden anxieties and triggers. Understanding your past and identifying fear-based thoughts were crucial steps toward building self-awareness.

Then, we focused on improving relationship dynamics through effective communication, building trust, navigating conflicts, and setting healthy boundaries. We also covered balancing professional and personal life with productivity hacks, delegation techniques, and strategies for managing workplace stress. And let's not forget the importance of managing technology and digital distractions.

Parenting without control was another significant topic, emphasizing setting healthy boundaries, encouraging independence, and creating a nurturing home environment. Navigating societal and cultural pressures helped you break free from traditional roles and embrace your authentic self. Building a support network and embracing flexibility and adaptability rounded out our journey, giving you the tools to navigate life's challenges with grace and resilience.

Key Takeaways:

- **Self-Awareness:** Understanding and recognizing control behaviors is the first step toward change.
- **Practical Tools:** Mindfulness, deep-breathing exercises, and CBT can significantly reduce anxiety and stress.
- **Healthy Relationships:** Effective communication, trust-building, and setting boundaries are essential for healthy relationships.
- **Work-Life Balance:** Productivity hacks, delegation, and managing workplace stress can help you balance your professional and personal life.
- **Parental Guidance:** Setting healthy boundaries and encouraging independence in your children fosters a nurturing environment.
- **Societal Pressures:** Breaking free from traditional roles and embracing your authentic self is empowering.
- **Support Networks:** Building and maintaining a support network is crucial for ongoing growth and resilience.
- **Flexibility:** Embracing flexibility and adaptability helps you navigate life's changes with ease.

Now, it's time for a call to action. Take a moment to reflect on what you've learned and how it applies to your life. What small steps can you take today to start releasing control and embracing a more balanced, fulfilling life? Maybe it's delegating a task at work, practicing mindfulness for a few minutes each day, or setting a new boundary in a relationship. Whatever it is, commit to taking that first step.

Remember, change doesn't happen overnight. It's a journey, and every step you take, no matter how small, is progress. Be kind to yourself, celebrate your achievements, and don't be afraid to ask for help when needed. I'm here to support you every step of the way. Whether it's through continued reading, joining a support group, or seeking professional help, know that you're not alone.

In closing, I want to leave you with an empowering note: You have the power to change your life. You can achieve a more balanced, fulfilling life by releasing control, enhancing self-awareness, and nurturing emotional growth. Your relationships will flourish, your mental health will improve, and you'll find a newfound sense of peace and joy. Embrace this journey with an open heart and mind, and remember that every step you take brings you closer to the life you deserve.

Keep going, and never forget that you're stronger and more capable than you realize. The path to a more balanced, fulfilling life is within your reach. You've got this!

References

- The Origins and Future of Control Theory in Psychology https://journals.sagepub.com/doi/10.1037/gpr0000057
- The relationship between self-control and mental ... NCBI
- https://www.ncbi.nlm.nih.gov/pmc/articles/PMC10644003/#:~:text=Self%2Dcontrol%20is%20often%20associated,under%2Dcontrol%20(24)
- Controlling People: 12 Signs to Watch For
- https://www.healthline.com/health/controlling-people
- Controlling Behavior: 7 Signs To Look For https://www.webmd.com/mental-health/signs-controlling-behavior
- 5 mindfulness techniques for letting go of control https://www.fastcompany.com/90424137/5-mindfulness-techniques-for-letting-go-of-control
- Breathing Techniques for Stress Relief https://www.webmd.com/balance/stress-management/stress-relief-breathing-techniques
- 10 Strategies for Better Time Management https://extension.uga.edu/publications/detail.html?number=C1042&title=time-management-10-strategies-for-better-time-management
- 7 Ways to Set Realistic Expectations for Yourself https://psychcentral.com/health/suggestions-for-setting-realistic-expectations-with-yourself
- How Cognitive Behavioral Therapy Can Treat Your Anxiety https://www.healthline.com/health/anxiety/cbt-for-anxiety
- Women and Stress
- https://my.clevelandclinic.org/health/articles/5545-women-and-stress
- Mental Health and Sleep
- https://www.sleepfoundation.org/mental-health
- Nutritional psychiatry: Your brain on food https://www.health.harvard.edu/blog/nutritional-psychiatry-your-brain-on-food-201511168626
- The Power of Journaling for Well-being: A Path to Self ... https://dhwblog.dukehealth.org/the-power-of-journaling-for-well-being-a-path-to-self-discovery-and-healing/#:~:text=It%20offers%20the%20benefits%20of,happier%20and%20more%20balanced%20life
- 87 Self-Reflection Questions for Introspection [+Exercises] https://positivepsychology.com/introspection-self-reflection/
- How to Identify and Manage Your Emotional Triggers https://www.healthline.com/health/mental-health/emotional-triggers

- Understanding the Impact of Trauma - NCBI
- https://www.ncbi.nlm.nih.gov/books/NBK207191/
- 7 Keys to Effective Communication Skills in Relationships https://seattlechristiancounseling.com/articles/7-keys-to-effective-communication-skills-in-relationships
- How to Build Trust in a Relationship, According to a Therapist https://www.verywellmind.com/how-to-build-trust-in-a-relationship-5207611
- How Emotion Regulation Can Transform Your Conflict Cycle https://www.gottman.com/blog/emotion-regulation-transform-your-conflict-cycle/
- 7 Active Listening Techniques For Better Communication https://www.verywellmind.com/what-is-active-listening-3024343
- 5 Productivity Apps Every Working Mom Should Know About https://womenlovetech.com/5-productivity-apps-every-working-mom-should-know-about/
- How to Delegate Effectively: 9 Tips for Managers - HBS Online https://online.hbs.edu/blog/post/how-to-delegate-effectively
- Nine Strategies Busy Professionals Can Use To Reduce ... https://www.forbes.com/sites/forbescoachescouncil/2017/08/11/nine-strategies-busy-professionals-can-use-to-reduce-stress/
- 10 Work Life Balance Tips for Women https://www.moneylion.com/learn/10-work-life-balance-tips-for-women/
- Setting Healthy Boundaries for Kids: Why and How to Do It https://calmerry.com/blog/parenting/how-to-set-boundaries-for-children-without-yelling-threats-and-bribes/
- Promoting children's independence: What parents say vs do https://mottpoll.org/reports/promoting-childrens-independence-what-parents-say-vs-do
- Positive Reinforcement for Kids: 11+ Examples for Parents https://positivepsychology.com/parenting-positive-reinforcement/
- Parenting Stress and Self-Care https://getparentingtips.com/parents/health/parenting-stress-and-self-care/
- Understanding Gender Roles and Their Effect On Our ... https://www.verywellmind.com/understanding-gender-roles-and-their-effect-on-our-relationships-7499408
- Challenging Societal Expectations: Stories of Resilient ... https://www.becomebraveenough.com/blog/challenging-societal-expectations-stories-of-resilient-women

- Understanding 'Societal Expectations' and Stereotypes
  https://www.linkedin.com/pulse/understanding-societal-expectations-stereotypes-kim-jones-zcaxf

Women Embracing Peace

MINDFULNESS AND MEDITATION PRACTICES
TO RELEASE CONTROL, REDUCE STRESS,
REGULATE EMOTIONS, AND EMBRACE SELF-
COMPASSION FOR HOLISTIC WELL-BEING

Introduction

A few years ago, I sat in my car, gripping the steering wheel, tears streaming down my face. I had just left yet another stressful meeting where my perfectionism had been both my driving force and my undoing. I was exhausted, anxious, and overwhelmed. I realized that something had to change. This was my breaking point but also the beginning of a new journey. It was the moment I discovered mindfulness and meditation.

I started with small steps—pausing to take deep breaths, practicing gratitude, and eventually meditating for a few minutes each day. Slowly, I began to notice changes. My anxiety lessened, my need for control diminished, and I started to feel a sense of inner peace that I had never known before.

Many of us struggle with anxiety, perfectionism, and stress. We juggle multiple roles—mother, daughter, professional, friend—and often feel like we're failing. We set impossibly high standards for ourselves and feel crushed when we inevitably fall short. It's a cycle that can leave us feeling exhausted and inadequate.

That's where mindfulness and meditation come in. These practices offer a way to break the cycle. They help us find emotional balance, reduce stress, and overcome the crippling need for perfection. They teach us to be present in the moment and to accept ourselves just as we are.

The vision for "Women Embracing Peace" is to empower you to cultivate a life of emotional balance, inner calm, and self-acceptance through mindfulness practice. This book is not just another self-help guide. It's a supportive space to prioritize your emotional well-being, rediscover your inner strength, and find lasting peace.

This book is for you. Whether you are struggling with anxiety, feeling overwhelmed by the need for control, or constantly striving for perfection, this book is for you. It's for women who want to manage their mental health and embrace imperfection. It's for those who wish to release the need for control and find peace in the present moment.

The book is organized into several sections, each designed to guide you through different aspects of mindfulness and meditation. You'll find chapters on self-compassion, practical mindfulness techniques, emotional regulation, and living in the present moment. Each section includes personal stories, guided meditations, and real-life examples to help you apply these practices to your own life.

By working through this book, you will gain practical tools to manage your anxiety and stress. You will learn guided meditations to help you find calm and balance. You will read personal stories that show you are not alone in your struggles. You will find real-life examples demonstrating mindfulness's power in everyday life.

I encourage you to engage actively with this book. Try the exercises, reflect on the stories, and permit yourself to be imperfect. This journey is not about achieving perfection but finding peace and balance in imperfection.

So, dear reader, I invite you to join me on this journey towards inner peace and emotional resilience. Together, we will explore the power of mindfulness and meditation. We will uncover the strength within ourselves, embrace our imperfections, and find peace in the present moment.

Welcome to "Women Embracing Peace." Let's begin this journey together.

ONE

Embracing Self-Compassion

I remember a time when I was my harshest critic. I would look in the mirror and only see flaws. Every mistake felt like a monumental failure, and I carried the constant weight of not being good enough. During one particularly tough period, after a string of sleepless nights and countless bouts of self-doubt, I stumbled upon the concept of self-compassion. It was a lifeline I didn't know I needed. Self-compassion transformed my relationship with myself and, as a result, my entire life. Now, I want to share this powerful tool with you.

Understanding Self-Compassion

Self-compassion is about treating yourself with the same kindness and understanding you would offer a close friend. It involves three key components: self-kindness, common humanity, and mindfulness. Self-kindness means being gentle and understanding with yourself rather than harshly critical. Common humanity involves recognizing that everyone makes mistakes and has flaws.

Finally, mindfulness requires being present with your feelings and thoughts without over-identifying or pushing them away.

You might wonder how self-compassion differs from self-esteem. While self-esteem is about evaluating yourself positively, often compared to others, self-compassion isn't about judging yourself. It's about embracing yourself as you are, imperfections and all. This difference is crucial because self-esteem can sometimes lead to narcissism or an inflated sense of self-importance. In contrast, self-compassion fosters a balanced view of oneself, free from the extremes of self-criticism or self-importance.

The psychological benefits of self-compassion are profound. Research by Dr. Kristin Neff, a pioneer in the field, shows that self-compassion is linked to lower levels of anxiety and depression. It enhances emotional resilience, helping you bounce back from setbacks more easily. Neff's studies also reveal that self-compassionate people tend to have healthier relationships and a greater sense of well-being. They're more likely to engage in constructive behaviors and less likely to suffer from stress-related issues.

For example, one study found that self-compassionate individuals are better at handling failure. Instead of spiraling into self-loathing, they acknowledge their mistakes and move forward. This approach reduces the emotional toll of failure and encourages a growth mindset. Another study showed that self-compassion can improve mental health by reducing rumination, which is the tendency to dwell on negative thoughts. By practicing self-compassion, you can break the cycle of negative thinking and cultivate a more positive and balanced mental state.

Despite its benefits, self-compassion is often misunderstood. One common myth is that self-compassion is a form of self-pity. However, self-compassion is the opposite of self-pity. While self-pity involves wallowing in your problems and feeling isolated, self-compassion involves recognizing your struggles and acknowledging that everyone experiences difficulties. This recognition fosters a sense of connection rather than isolation.

Another misconception is that self-compassion will make you lazy or complacent. In reality, self-compassion motivates you to improve yourself healthily. Treating yourself with kindness makes you more likely to take care of your health, set realistic goals, and pursue your passions. Self-compassion encourages you to strive for excellence without the fear of failure that perfectionism brings.

Some people believe that self-compassion is selfish. They worry that focusing on their own needs will make them neglect others. However, self-compassion enhances your ability to care for others. When you meet your own emotional needs, you're less likely to experience burnout and more able to offer genuine support to those around you. Self-compassion builds a foundation of emotional stability from which you can better connect with and help others.

Take a moment to reflect on your current level of self-compassion. How do you typically respond to your own mistakes or shortcomings? Are you kind to yourself, or tend to be overly critical? Consider keeping a journal to explore these questions. Write about a recent situation where you were hard on yourself and think about how you could respond with more self-compassion in the future.

You might find it helpful to write about your feelings and reactions in detail. Journaling can help you identify patterns in your self-talk and offer insights into how you treat yourself. Reflect on whether your self-criticism is helping or hindering you. Often, we find that harsh self-criticism only adds to our stress and anxiety, while self-compassion opens the door to healing and growth.

By understanding and practicing self-compassion, you can transform your relationship with yourself and learn to navigate life's challenges with greater ease and resilience. This chapter will guide you through this transformative process, offering practical tools and insights to help you embrace self-compassion and unlock your inner peace.

Breaking Free from Perfectionism

Perfectionism is a sneaky companion. It often wears the mask of ambition and high standards, but underneath, it harbors a relentless inner critic. Recognizing perfectionist tendencies in your thoughts and behaviors is the first step toward breaking free. You might find yourself constantly setting unrealistically high expectations, feeling a persistent fear of failure, or being overly critical of your performance. Perfectionists often procrastinate, not wanting to start a task unless they can do it perfectly, and they frequently seek validation from others. These tendencies are not just quirks; they are deeply ingrained habits that can contribute to chronic anxiety.

The connection between perfectionism and anxiety is well-documented. When you set impossible standards for yourself, you create a fertile ground for anxiety to flourish. Perfectionism feeds a cycle of stress and self-doubt. You might constantly worry about making mistakes, which leads to a heightened state of alertness and stress. This anxiety, in turn, reinforces the need to be perfect, creating a vicious loop. Consider the example of a woman who spends hours perfecting a presentation. Despite her efforts, she feels it's never good enough and stays up late, tweaking it until she's exhausted. This constant striving for perfection leaves her feeling drained and anxious, never satisfied with her work.

The costs of perfectionism are steep. Emotionally, it can lead to burnout, inadequacy, and persistent dissatisfaction. Perfectionism can strain personal relationships as well. Holding yourself to impossible standards might inadvertently project those expectations onto others, leading to frustration and conflict. Professionally, perfectionism can be equally damaging. It can cause you to miss deadlines due to excessive work refining or avoid taking on new challenges for fear of failing to meet your high standards. Physically, the stress associated with perfectionism can manifest as headaches, insomnia, or other stress-related ailments.

Overcoming perfectionism requires practical strategies and a shift in mindset. One effective approach is setting realistic goals. Instead of aiming for perfection, set achievable and specific goals. Break tasks into smaller, manageable steps and celebrate progress rather than perfection. Embrace mistakes as learning opportunities. Understand that making mistakes is a natural part of growth and development. Each mistake teaches a valuable lesson that can guide you toward improvement. Practicing self-forgiveness is crucial. When you fall short of your expectations, offer words of kindness and understanding instead of berating yourself, recognizing that it's okay to be imperfect.

Let me share some inspiring stories of women who have successfully overcome perfectionism through self-compassion. One high-achieving executive used to lose sleep over every minor error in her reports. By learning to set realistic goals and practicing self-forgiveness, she found a balance that allowed her to excel without burning out. She began to see mistakes as opportunities for growth rather than as failures. Another woman, a dedicated teacher, struggled with perfectionism in her classroom. She felt she had to be the perfect teacher to earn her students' respect. By embracing self-compassion, she learned to accept her imperfections and focus on the joy of teaching rather than the pressure of perfection.

In the workplace, perfectionism can be particularly challenging. I remember working with a colleague who was a textbook perfectionist. She would spend countless hours on projects, often missing deadlines because she was never satisfied with her work. This led to immense stress and strained relationships with her team. She learned to manage her perfectionist tendencies through self-compassion and setting realistic goals. She started to delegate tasks, trust her team, and accept that "good enough" was often more effective than perfect. This shift improved her well-being and enhanced her productivity and team dynamics.

I have battled with perfectionism in various facets of life. I used to believe everything had to be flawless before I could consider it complete. Whether it was a work project, a home improvement task, or even writing this book, the pressure to be perfect was relentless. It wasn't until I started practicing self-compassion that I realized the toll perfectionism was taking on my mental and physical health. By setting realistic goals and embracing my imperfections, I found a sense of peace and fulfillment that perfectionism could never offer. The journey is ongoing, but each step toward self-compassion brings more balance and joy into my life.

Cultivating a Kind Inner Voice

We all have an inner critic. That nagging voice tells you you must be better, smart, or capable enough. This inner critic can be relentless, undermining your self-worth and your confidence. Understanding this inner critic is the first step in transforming it into a kinder, more supportive voice.

The inner critic often has distinct characteristics. It's judgmental, harsh, and unforgiving. It thrives on comparing you to others and magnifying your flaws. This critical voice usually originates from early experiences, perhaps from critical parents, teachers, or societal expectations. Over time, these external critiques become internalized, forming a persistent negative self-talk that affects your self-worth.

The impact of the inner critic on self-worth can be profound. Constant self-criticism can lead to feelings of inadequacy and low self-esteem. It can make you doubt your abilities and hesitate to take risks. This negative self-talk can become a barrier to personal growth and happiness, trapping you in a cycle of self-doubt and discouragement.

But you can transform this negative self-talk into compassionate and supportive self-talk. The first step is identifying negative thought patterns. Pay attention to the language your inner critic uses. Is it filled with words like "always" and "never"? Does it focus on your failures and ignore your successes? Recognizing these patterns is crucial to changing them.

Once you've identified negative thoughts, work on reframing them. Instead of saying, "I always mess things up," try, "I made a mistake, but I can learn from it." Reframing helps shift the focus from self-blame to self-improvement. It's about turning critical thoughts into constructive ones that encourage growth rather than hinder it.

Practicing positive affirmations can also help. Positive affirmations are statements that reinforce positive beliefs about yourself. They might initially feel awkward, but with practice, they can become a powerful tool for transforming self-talk. Try affirmations like, "I am worthy of love and respect," or "I am capable and strong." Repeat them daily, and notice how they begin to shift your mindset.

Mindfulness is crucial in noticing self-critical thoughts and replacing them with kind words. Mindfulness involves observing your thoughts without judgment. When you practice mindfulness, you create a space between your thoughts and reactions, allowing you to choose a more compassionate response. One effective mindfulness technique is to simply observe your thoughts as they arise without getting caught up in them.

Exercises for practicing self-kindness in the moment can be incredibly helpful. When you notice self-critical thoughts, pause and take a few deep breaths. Remind yourself that it's okay to be imperfect. Place your hand on your heart and offer yourself words of kindness, just as you would to a dear friend. This simple gesture can help shift your mindset from self-criticism to self-compassion.

Incorporating daily mindfulness practices can also support a kinder inner voice. Set aside a few minutes each day for a mindfulness meditation. Focus on your breath and gently bring your attention back whenever your mind wanders. Over time, this practice can help you develop greater awareness of your thoughts and create a habit of self-compassion.

Practical Exercise: Loving-Kindness Meditation

One powerful exercise to cultivate a kind inner voice is the loving-kindness meditation. Find a quiet place where you won't be disturbed. Sit comfortably and close your eyes. Take a few deep breaths to center yourself. Begin by silently repeating loving-kind phrases to yourself, such as "May I be happy. May I be healthy. May I be safe. May I live with ease." Feel the warmth and compassion these words bring. After a few minutes, extend these wishes to others, starting with loved ones and gradually including neutral people and even difficult individuals. This practice can help develop a sense of compassion for yourself and others, fostering a kinder inner dialogue.

Another effective practice is self-compassion letter writing. Write a letter to yourself as if you were writing to a close friend who is struggling. Use kind and encouraging words. Acknowledge your struggles, but also remind yourself of your strengths and the progress you've made. This exercise can provide a tangible reminder of your self-worth and the importance of self-compassion.

Affirmation journaling is another great way to cultivate a kind inner voice. Each day, write down a few positive affirmations about yourself. Reflect on them and notice how they make you feel. Over time, this practice can help reinforce positive beliefs and diminish the inner critic's power.

By understanding and transforming your inner critic, you can cultivate a kind inner voice that supports your growth and well-being. This shift can profoundly impact your mental and emotional health, helping you navigate life with greater self-compassion and resilience.

Self-Compassion Exercises for Daily Life

Incorporating self-compassion into your daily routine can be a game-changer. Simple rituals and practices can create a foundation of kindness and understanding towards yourself. Let's explore practical ways to make self-compassion a part of your everyday life.

Daily Self-Compassion Rituals

Starting your day with self-compassion affirmations can set a positive tone. As you wake up each morning, speak kindly to yourself for a few moments. Say things like, "I am worthy of love and respect," or "I am enough, just as I am." These affirmations may initially feel strange, but with time, they can shift your mindset and help you approach the day with a compassionate heart.

In the evening, reflect on your day with a gratitude practice. As you lie in bed, think about three things you are grateful for. They can be small, like a warm cup of tea, or significant, like a supportive friend. This practice helps you end the day positively and reinforces self-compassion by focusing on the good in your life rather than what went wrong.

Midday self-check-ins are also crucial. During a busy day, pause to ask yourself how you're feeling. Are you stressed, tired, or anxious? Acknowledge these feelings without judgment and offer yourself some kindness. You might say, "It's okay to feel this way. I'm doing my best." This simple act of checking in can prevent stress and remind you to treat yourself compassionately.

Mindful Self-Compassion Practices

Taking self-compassion breaks throughout the day can help you stay grounded. Find a quiet space, close your eyes, and take a few deep breaths. Remind yourself that taking a break is okay and that your well-being matters. These short breaks can recharge your energy and provide peace on a hectic day.

Mindful breathing exercises are another powerful tool. When you feel overwhelmed, focus on your breath for a few minutes. Inhale deeply through your nose, hold for a few seconds, and exhale slowly through your mouth. This practice can calm your mind and body, allowing you to approach challenges with a clearer perspective.

A body scan for self-compassion can also be incredibly soothing. Lie comfortably and slowly bring your attention to each body part, starting from your toes and moving up to your head. As you focus on each area, send it kindness and gratitude. This practice helps you connect with your body and cultivate a sense of self-compassion.

Integrating Self-Compassion at Work

Work can be a breeding ground for stress and self-criticism. Practicing self-compassion in a professional setting is vital. Start by setting boundaries and learning to say no when necessary. It's okay to decline additional tasks if you're already overwhelmed. Saying no can be an act of self-compassion, allowing you to protect your well-being and maintain a healthy work-life balance.

In stressful situations, remind yourself to practice self-compassion. If you make a mistake or face criticism, take a moment to breathe and offer yourself understanding. Remember that everyone makes mistakes, and it's part of being human. A self-compassionate mindset can help you navigate challenges with resilience and grace.

Be a role model to encourage a self-compassionate work culture. Share your practices with colleagues and create an environment where it's okay to be imperfect. By showing kindness to yourself and others, you contribute to a supportive and compassionate workplace.

Building a Support System

Surrounding yourself with supportive people is crucial for fostering self-compassion. Identify individuals in your life who encourage and uplift you. These could be friends, family members, or colleagues who understand the importance of self-compassion and support your journey.

Setting healthy boundaries with unsupportive people is also essential. It's okay to distance yourself from those who bring negativity into your life. Protecting your emotional well-being is a form of self-compassion, and it's important to prioritize relationships that nourish you.

Creating a self-compassion support group can be incredibly beneficial. Find a few like-minded individuals who are also interested in practicing self-compassion. Meet regularly to share experiences, discuss challenges, and support each other. This group can provide a sense of community and accountability, making it easier to maintain your self-compassion practices.

Incorporating these self-compassion exercises into your daily life can transform how you treat yourself. By cultivating kindness and understanding, you can easily navigate challenges and foster inner peace. Remember, self-compassion is not a one-time act but a continuous practice that grows stronger. Embrace these practices and allow yourself to thrive.

TWO

Mindfulness Fundamentals

I remember a moment vividly from a few years ago. I was sitting in my living room, surrounded by a sea of papers and to-do lists. My mind was racing, my heart was pounding, and I felt like I was drowning in my own life. A friend mentioned mindfulness to me before, but I had brushed it off as another trend. But in that moment of overwhelming chaos, I decided to try it. I closed my eyes, took a deep breath, and focused on the feeling of the air filling my lungs. I felt a tiny spark of calm for the first time in what felt like forever. This was my first step into the world of mindfulness, and it changed everything.

What is Mindfulness?

Mindfulness is simply paying attention to the present moment without judgment. It sounds straightforward, but it's incredibly powerful. Rooted in Buddhist meditation practices, mindfulness has been around for thousands of years. These practices were designed to cultivate a deep awareness of the mind and body, helping practitioners live in harmony with themselves and the world around them.

In recent decades, mindfulness has been adapted into Western psychology. Researchers and therapists have recognized its benefits for mental health, integrating mindfulness into various therapeutic approaches. Programs like Mindfulness-Based Stress Reduction (MBSR) and Mindfulness-Based Cognitive Therapy (MBCT) have become popular tools for managing stress, anxiety, and depression. The beauty of mindfulness lies in its simplicity and accessibility—anyone can practice it anywhere, anytime.

At its core, mindfulness involves three principles: present-moment awareness, nonjudgmental observation, and acceptance. Present-moment awareness means focusing on what's happening now rather than dwelling on the past or worrying about the future. For example, when you're washing dishes, you might focus on the sensation of the warm water on your hands and the sound of the water splashing.

Non-judgmental observation involves noticing your thoughts, feelings, and sensations without labeling them good or bad. This can be challenging, especially if you're used to being self-critical. But with practice, you can learn to observe your inner experiences with curiosity and kindness. Imagine you're feeling anxious about an upcoming presentation. Instead of criticizing yourself for being nervous, you can simply acknowledge and observe the anxiety without judgment.

Acceptance is about letting go of the need to control everything and allowing things to be as they are. This doesn't mean giving up or being passive. Instead, it's about recognizing what you can't change and focusing your energy on what you can. For instance, if you're stuck in traffic and running late, you can accept the situation and use the time to practice mindful breathing rather than getting frustrated.

Many people confuse mindfulness with meditation, but they're not quite the same. Meditation is a broader practice that includes various techniques for calming the mind and achieving a state of deep relaxation or heightened awareness. Mindfulness is a specific type of meditation that focuses on present-moment awareness. While all mindfulness practices are a form of meditation, not all meditation practices are mindfulness-based.

There are countless ways to practice mindfulness beyond traditional meditation. Mindful walking is one example. Instead of rushing from place to place, try walking slowly and paying attention to each step. Notice the sensation of your feet touching the ground, the rhythm of your breath, and the sights and sounds around you. This simple practice can transform an ordinary walk into a calming, grounding experience.

Mindful listening is another powerful practice. Focus fully on the other person without planning your response or getting distracted when conversing. Listen with an open heart and mind, and notice how this deepens your connection with the other person. This practice enhances your relationships and brings a sense of presence and calm to your interactions.

Mindful eating is a practice that can transform your relationship with food. Instead of eating on autopilot, take the time to savor each bite. Notice the flavors, textures, and aromas of your food. Pay attention to how your body feels as you eat, and stop when satisfied. This practice can help you develop a healthier, more mindful approach to eating and reduce stress around food.

Incorporating mindfulness into your daily activities can profoundly impact your well-being. You don't need to set aside a specific time for mindfulness; you can weave it into your everyday life. Whether brushing your teeth, drinking tea, or folding laundry, you can practice mindfulness by focusing fully on the task.

By understanding and practicing mindfulness, you can find peace and balance amid life's challenges. It's a powerful tool for managing anxiety, controlling perfectionist tendencies, and cultivating inner peace. So, take a deep breath, and let's explore the transformative power of mindfulness together.

The Science Behind Mindfulness

The benefits of mindfulness are anecdotal and backed by solid scientific evidence. Harvard researchers, for instance, have been delving into the effects of mindfulness on brain function. Their studies show that mindfulness can bring about significant changes in the brain, particularly in areas associated with emotional regulation and stress. Functional magnetic resonance imaging (fMRI) scans reveal that regular mindfulness practice can reduce activity in the amygdala, the part of the brain responsible for our fight-or-flight response. This reduction in activity translates to lower stress levels and a calmer state of mind.

Moreover, the research continues beyond there. Studies have shown that mindfulness can enhance activity in the prefrontal cortex, the area of the brain responsible for executive functions like decision-making, focus, and self-control. This enhancement helps you stay more present and make better decisions, reducing the chaos that often fuels anxiety and perfectionism. Neuroscientific evidence also points to neuroplasticity, the brain's ability to reorganize itself by forming new neural connections. Mindfulness practices can promote neuroplasticity, making adopting healthier habits and thought patterns easier.

When it comes to health benefits, mindfulness offers a range of advantages. Scientific research has demonstrated that mindfulness can help reduce chronic pain. By teaching you to observe pain without judgment, mindfulness allows you to change your relationship with it, reducing its intensity. Studies also indicate that mindfulness can boost your immune function. A stronger immune system means you're less likely to fall ill, which can be a game-changer if you constantly battle stress-related ailments. Additionally, mindfulness is known to improve sleep quality. Better sleep leads to better overall health, making it easier to manage anxiety and stress.

The psychological benefits of mindfulness are equally compelling. Numerous studies have shown that mindfulness can significantly decrease symptoms of depression and anxiety. By fostering a non-judgmental awareness of your thoughts and feelings, mindfulness helps you break the cycle of negative thinking that often accompanies these conditions. Emotional resilience is another key benefit. Mindfulness practices teach you to observe your emotions without getting swept away, allowing you to respond to challenges more effectively. This increased emotional resilience can make a world of difference when dealing with the pressures of daily life.

Moreover, mindfulness can contribute to an overall sense of well-being. When you're more present and less worried about the past or future, you can better enjoy the moments that make life meaningful. This heightened well-being can enhance relationships, improve work performance, and make everyday activities more enjoyable. It's not just about reducing stress; it's about holistically enriching your life.

The Harvard Gazette reports that public interest in mindfulness has skyrocketed, and for good reason. Mindfulness-based interventions (MBIs) are increasingly used to treat a variety of psychological conditions, from stress and anxiety to chronic pain and depression. A growing body of research supports these interventions and highlights their effectiveness. For instance, MBIs have been shown to improve emotion regulation by enhancing both top-down and bottom-up mechanisms. This dual approach helps you manage your emotions more effectively, reducing the likelihood of emotional outbursts or prolonged periods of distress.

Neuroscientific studies also reveal that mindfulness impacts several brain regions involved in attention, emotional regulation, and self-referential processing. These include the insula, responsible for body awareness, and the anterior cingulate cortex, which plays a role in emotion regulation. By practicing mindfulness, you can change the structure and function of your brain, making it easier to manage stress and maintain emotional balance.

Regarding practical applications, mindfulness training modifies neural processes in the three attention networks: alerting, orienting, and executive control. This modification helps you stay focused and attentive, making managing tasks easier and reducing the overwhelm that often accompanies perfectionism. The changes in brain function are not just temporary; they persist even when you're not actively meditating. This means that the benefits of mindfulness extend beyond your practice sessions, enriching your daily life in meaningful ways.

So, let's talk about how all this scientific evidence translates into real-world benefits. Imagine you're at work, juggling multiple deadlines, and feeling the pressure to perform perfectly. Mindfulness can activate your prefrontal cortex, helping you stay focused and make better decisions. This can reduce your stress levels and improve your performance, making it easier to meet your deadlines without feeling overwhelmed. Or consider a situation where you're dealing with chronic pain. Mindfulness can help you observe the pain without judgment, reducing its intensity and making it easier to cope.

The Benefits of Mindful Living

When you start embracing mindfulness, one of the first things you may notice is an improvement in your emotional well-being. Mindfulness helps you regulate your emotions more effectively, making navigating life's ups and downs easier. Techniques like mindful breathing and body scans can help you observe your emotions without getting swept away. For instance, when you feel a wave of anxiety coming on, instead of letting it take over, you can take a moment to focus on your breath, acknowledging the anxiety without judgment. This simple practice can create a space between you and your emotions, allowing you to respond more calmly and thoughtfully.

Let's look at some real-life examples. Take Jamie, a high-powered executive who struggled with stress and anxiety. After incorporating mindfulness into her daily routine, she was less reactive and more composed during high-stress meetings. She began to use mindful breathing techniques whenever she felt overwhelmed, which helped her maintain her composure and make better decisions. Similarly, a teacher, Mikayla, used mindfulness to manage her stress levels during the school day. She could stay grounded and present by taking short mindfulness breaks between classes, improving her interactions with students and colleagues.

Mindfulness also significantly enhances focus and concentration, benefiting your personal and professional life. Training your mind to stay in the present moment can reduce distractions and improve your ability to concentrate on tasks. One simple exercise to improve concentration is the practice of mindful observation. Pick an object, like a flower or a piece of fruit, and spend a few minutes observing it in detail. Notice its colors, textures, and shapes. This exercise can help train your mind to focus and is particularly helpful if you struggle with maintaining attention at work.

Consider the case of Katelyn, a writer who found it challenging to focus on her projects due to constant distractions. She improved her concentration and productivity by integrating mindfulness practices into her routine. She started her day with a short meditation session and used mindful breaks to reset her focus. This practice not only boosted her productivity but also enhanced the quality of her work. Similarly, Meghan, a software engineer, used mindfulness to improve her focus during coding sessions. She could work more efficiently and clearly by practicing mindful breathing before starting her tasks.

Enhanced relationships are another significant benefit of mindful living. Mindfulness fosters empathy, active listening, and emotional understanding, which are crucial for healthy relationships. Mindful communication techniques, such as active listening and non-judgmental observation, can improve your interactions with others. When you practice mindful communication, you focus entirely on the other person, listening to their words without planning your response or getting distracted. This deep level of attentiveness can strengthen your connections and improve your relationships.

Take the example of Brooke and her husband struggling with communication issues. By incorporating mindfulness practices into their interactions, they improved their understanding of each other's perspectives. They practiced active listening during their conversations, which helped them feel more connected and supported. Similarly, Danielle used mindfulness to improve her relationship with her teenage daughter. She created a more open and supportive environment for their conversations by practicing non-judgmental observation and empathy.

The overall quality of life also improves when you embrace mindful living. Mindfulness helps you find balance and fulfillment in your daily activities, making life more enjoyable and meaningful. Testimonials from individuals who practice mindfulness often highlight its profound impact on their overall well-being. For example, a busy professional, Sidney found that mindfulness helped her achieve a better work-life balance. By incorporating mindfulness into her daily routine, she was able to reduce stress and find more joy in his personal life.

Practical tips for integrating mindfulness into daily life can make a significant difference. Start by setting aside a few minutes each day for mindfulness practice. You can begin with short sessions and gradually increase the duration as you become more comfortable. Incorporate mindfulness into everyday activities, such as eating, walking, or household chores. The key is to be fully present in whatever you are doing, focusing on the sensations and experiences of the moment.

By embracing mindful living, you can enhance your emotional well-being, improve your focus and concentration, foster healthier relationships, and achieve a higher overall quality of life. Mindfulness is not just a practice; it's a way of living that can transform every aspect of your life. So take a deep breath, be present, and start experiencing the countless benefits of mindful living today.

Dispelling Myths About Mindfulness

One common misconception is that mindfulness is inherently religious. While it's true that mindfulness has historical roots in Buddhist meditation practices, it has been adapted into a secular context that makes it accessible to everyone. In its modern form, mindfulness is about paying attention to the present moment without judgment and doesn't require any particular spiritual belief. Secular mindfulness programs like Mindfulness-Based Stress Reduction (MBSR) and Mindfulness-Based Cognitive Therapy (MBCT) have been developed to help people manage stress, anxiety, and other mental health issues. These programs are used in hospitals, schools, and workplaces worldwide, making mindfulness a universal tool for well-being. Testimonials from people of diverse spiritual backgrounds show that mindfulness can complement various belief systems rather than conflict with them. Whether you're religious, spiritual, or neither, mindfulness offers practical benefits that anyone can enjoy.

Another myth is that mindfulness requires a lot of time. Many people think they must dedicate hours daily to practice mindfulness effectively, but this isn't true. Even brief practices can be incredibly effective. You can start with just five minutes a day. Simple exercises like mindful breathing or a quick body scan can fit easily into your busy schedule. Take, for instance, a working mom named Tenisha who juggles a demanding job and two kids. She found that practicing mindfulness for just a few minutes in the morning and evening significantly impacted her stress levels. Tips for integrating mindfulness into a busy schedule include setting reminders on your phone, practicing mindfulness during daily activities like brushing your teeth or waiting in line, and taking short, mindful breaks throughout the day. The key is consistency, not duration. Small, regular practices can lead to meaningful changes over time.

Many people also believe mindfulness is about clearing your mind of all thoughts. This is a misconception. Mindfulness is not about emptying your mind but observing your thoughts without judgment. It's natural for your mind to wander; the goal is to notice where it goes and gently bring it back to the present moment. Understanding the nature of thoughts can help you practice non-judgmental observation. Your thoughts are just mental events—they come and go like clouds in the sky. Techniques for non-judgmental observation include focusing on your breath, labeling your thoughts (e.g., "thinking" or "worrying"), and using a gentle, curious attitude toward your mental experiences. Personal stories of practicing mindful observation show that this approach can reduce the power of negative thoughts and increase emotional resilience. For example, Teresa, who struggled with chronic anxiety, found that observing her anxious thoughts without judgment helped her feel less overwhelmed and more in control.

Another myth is that mindfulness is only for naturally calm or serene individuals. This couldn't be further from the truth. Mindfulness is especially beneficial for people who experience high levels of stress or anxiety. It provides tools to navigate life's challenges with greater ease. Examples of high-stress individuals benefiting from mindfulness include first responders, military personnel, and busy professionals.

These people often face intense pressure and stress, yet mindfulness helps them stay grounded and focused. Techniques for practicing mindfulness amidst chaos include grounding exercises, mindful breathing, and using mindfulness apps to guide you through quick practices. Encouraging stories of transformation through mindfulness shows that it can bring significant benefits even in the most chaotic environments. Take Jenna, a nurse working in a busy hospital. Practicing mindfulness taught her to stay calm and centered during emergencies, improving her performance and reducing her stress levels.

By dispelling these myths, we open the door for everyone to experience the transformative power of mindfulness. It's not about adhering to a particular belief system, dedicating hours of your day, or achieving a state of thoughtless bliss. Mindfulness is for everyone, especially those navigating the complexities of modern life. With its practical applications and proven benefits, mindfulness can help you manage anxiety, control perfectionist tendencies, and find inner peace. In the next chapter, we'll delve into practical mindfulness techniques you can use immediately. These tools will help you integrate mindfulness into your daily routine, making it a natural part of your life.

THREE

Practical Mindfulness Techniques

Let's dive into some practical mindfulness techniques to help you manage anxiety, control, and perfectionism while deepening your inner peace.

Mindful Breathing Exercises

It all started with a breath. I remember one particularly chaotic day when everything seemed to spiral out of control. I felt like I was sinking into a sea of stress and anxiety. That's when a friend suggested I try mindful breathing. Skeptical but desperate, I decided to give it a shot. I closed my eyes, took a deep breath, and focused on the sensation of air filling my lungs. Something shifted within me. That single breath became an anchor, grounding me in the present moment and offering a brief respite from my racing thoughts.

Mindful breathing is the cornerstone of mindfulness practice. It involves paying attention to your breath, observing each inhale and exhale without trying to change it. The beauty of mindful breathing lies in its simplicity and accessibility. You don't need any special equipment or a quiet room. All you need is your breath, which is always with you. The basics of mindful breathing are straightforward: find a comfortable position, close your eyes if you feel comfortable, and focus on the sensation of breathing. Notice the cool air entering your nostrils and the warm air leaving. Feel your chest and belly rise and fall with each breath. If your mind wanders, gently bring it back to your breath without judgment.

Mindful breathing can significantly reduce stress and anxiety. When you focus on your breath, you bring your attention to the present moment, which can help break the cycle of anxious thoughts. Physiologically, mindful breathing activates the parasympathetic nervous system, which promotes relaxation. Deep, slow breaths signal to your body that it's safe to relax, reducing the production of stress hormones like cortisol. This physiological response can help lower your heart rate and blood pressure, creating a sense of calm and grounding.

Let's explore a few simple breathing techniques you can practice anytime, anywhere. The 4-7-8 breathing technique is a favorite of mine. It's simple yet powerful. Here's how it works: inhale through your nose for a count of four, hold your breath for seven, and exhale through your mouth for a count of eight. Repeat this cycle three to four times. This technique can help calm your mind and body, making it easier to manage anxiety and stress.

Another effective technique is box breathing, also known as square breathing. This method involves inhaling, holding, exhaling, and holding your breath again, each for a count of four. Imagine tracing the sides of a square as you breathe: inhale for four counts, hold for four, exhale for four, and hold again for four. This rhythmic breathing pattern can help regulate your breath and create a sense of balance and calm.

Alternate nostril breathing is a technique often used in yoga. It involves breathing in and out of one nostril at a time, alternating between them. Start by sitting comfortably. Close your right nostril with your right thumb and inhale deeply through your left nostril. Close your left nostril with your right ring finger and exhale through your right nostril. Inhale through your right nostril, then close it and exhale through your left nostril. Continue this pattern for a few minutes. Alternate nostril breathing can help balance your brain's left and right hemispheres, promoting mental clarity and emotional stability.

Deep breathing exercises can also help with relaxation and grounding. The diaphragm plays a crucial role in deep breathing. When you breathe deeply from your diaphragm rather than shallowly from your chest, you can access a deeper state of relaxation. To practice deep belly breathing, sit or lie down comfortably. Place one hand on your chest and the other on your belly. Take a slow, deep breath through your nose, allowing your belly to rise and push your hand out. Your chest should remain relatively still. Exhale slowly through your mouth, feeling your belly fall. Repeat this process for a few minutes, focusing on the rise and fall of your belly.

Integrating mindful breathing into your daily life can be incredibly beneficial. You can practice mindful breathing during work breaks to reset and recharge. Take a few minutes to step away from your desk, find a quiet spot, and focus on your breath. This can help you return to your tasks with renewed focus and calm. Using mindful breathing to start and end your day can also set a positive tone. Begin your morning with a few minutes of mindful breathing to center yourself before the day begins. Use mindful breathing to unwind and prepare for a restful sleep at night.

Mindful breathing can be a powerful tool to regain composure during stressful situations. If you find yourself feeling overwhelmed, take a moment to focus on your breath. Even a few deep, mindful breaths can create a sense of calm and help you navigate the situation with clarity and poise.

Practice Exercise: Quick Mindful Breathing Break

Take a moment right now to practice a quick, mindful breathing break. Find a comfortable position and close your eyes if you feel comfortable. Take a deep breath through your nose, allowing your belly to rise. Hold the breath for a count of three, then exhale slowly through your mouth, letting your belly fall. Repeat this process three times. Notice how you feel before and after the exercise. This quick break can be used anytime during your day to center yourself and find peace.

Mindful breathing is a simple yet powerful practice that can help you manage anxiety, control, and perfectionism. Incorporating these techniques into your daily life can create calm and grounding moments, deepening your inner peace.

Body Scan Meditation

It was one of those nights where sleep seemed impossible. My mind was racing, and my body was tense from the day's stress. I remembered hearing about body scan meditation from a mindfulness workshop I had attended, so I decided to try it. I lay down, closed my eyes, and focused on different body parts, starting from my toes and moving up to my head. As I paid attention to each area, I noticed the tension melting away and a sense of calm washing over me. That night, I slept better than I had in weeks.

Body scan meditation is a powerful technique that involves paying close attention to various parts of your body, one at a time. The purpose is to develop a greater mind-body connection, enhancing your awareness of physical sensations and how they relate to your mental and emotional state. This practice can help you identify areas of tension or discomfort, allowing you to address them before they escalate. The benefits of body scan meditation are numerous. It can significantly reduce stress and promote relaxation, making it easier to manage anxiety and perfectionist tendencies. You can cultivate a deeper inner peace and well-being by focusing on the present moment and observing your body's sensations without judgment.

To enhance the effectiveness of your body scan meditation, create a quiet and comfortable environment. Find a space where you won't be disturbed, and consider using soft lighting or calming scents like lavender to set the mood. Setting a regular practice schedule can also be beneficial. Consistency is key to reaping the full benefits of mindfulness practices. Aim to practice body scan meditation at the same time each day, whether in the morning to start your day calmly or in the evening to unwind before bed. Guided body scan recordings can be helpful, especially if you're new to the practice. Many apps and online resources offer guided meditations, providing gentle prompts to help you stay focused and present.

Body scan meditation can address common challenges in various real-life scenarios. For instance, it's an excellent tool for reducing tension and pain. If you experience chronic pain or muscle tension, regular body scan practice can help you become more aware of these sensations and manage them more effectively. It can also improve sleep quality. By practicing body scan meditation before bed, you can release the day's stress and prepare your mind and body for restful sleep. Additionally, body scan meditation can enhance focus and concentration. When you develop a habit of tuning into your body's sensations, you can carry this heightened awareness into other areas of your life, improving your ability to stay present and focused on tasks.

Practice Exercise: Body Scan Meditation

Find a quiet place where you won't be disturbed. Lie down or sit comfortably, and close your eyes. Take a few deep breaths to center yourself. Start by focusing on your toes. Notice any sensations, whether it's warmth, coolness, or tingling. Allow yourself to observe these sensations without judgment. Slowly move your attention up to your feet, then to your ankles, calves, knees, and so on, until you've scanned your entire body from head to toe. As you move through each part of your body, practice observing sensations without judgment. If you notice tension or discomfort, breathe into that area and visualize the tension melting away with each exhale. This practice can help you develop a more compassionate relationship with your body, recognizing that it's okay to experience discomfort and that you can address it mindfully.

Body scan meditation is a versatile and effective mindfulness practice that can help you manage anxiety, control, and perfectionism. Incorporating this technique into your daily routine can deepen your connection with your body, reduce stress, and cultivate inner peace.

Walking Meditation for Busy Lives

I remember when my days were so packed that finding a moment to sit quietly felt impossible. One day, a mentor suggested walking meditation—a revolutionary practice. Instead of trying to carve out time to sit still, I could integrate mindfulness into something I was already doing: walking. Walking meditation is a practice that combines the physical act of walking with the mental focus of meditation. It allows you to bring your body and mind into sync, creating a harmonious rhythm that can be incredibly grounding.

Walking meditation offers numerous benefits for both mental and physical health. It can reduce stress, improve mood, and enhance focus, much like traditional seated meditation. However, walking meditation also provides the added advantage of physical exercise. This makes it an excellent choice for busy individuals struggling to find time for physical activity and mindfulness. Walking meditation can be practiced almost anywhere, unlike seated meditation, which requires a quiet space and a certain amount of stillness. Walking through a bustling city or a tranquil park, you can transform your steps into a meditative practice.

To perform walking meditation, start by finding a suitable location. It could be a quiet path, a section of your office building, or even a hallway at home. The key is choosing a place to walk back and forth without too many distractions. Begin by standing still momentarily, taking a few deep breaths to center yourself. As you start walking, focus on the sensations of each step. Feel your feet touching the ground, notice the movement of your legs, and pay attention to the rhythm of your gait. Try to synchronize your breath with your steps. For example, inhale for four steps, then exhale for the next four. This rhythmic breathing can help you stay focused and present.

Incorporating walking meditation into your daily routine can be surprisingly easy. One effective way is to practice it during your daily commute. If you walk to work or use public transportation, focus on your steps and breath for a few minutes. This can transform a mundane commute into a calming, mindful experience. Using walking meditation during work breaks is another excellent option. Instead of scrolling through your phone or grabbing a coffee, take a short walk around your office building or nearby park. This practice can help clear your mind and improve your focus for the rest of the day. Combining walking meditation with nature walks can also be profoundly grounding. The natural environment can enhance your sense of presence and connection, making the practice even more powerful.

The broader concept of mindful movement extends beyond walking meditation, including activities like yoga and tai chi. These practices incorporate mindfulness into physical exercise, offering a holistic approach to well-being. Yoga, for example, combines physical postures with mindful breathing and meditation, promoting flexibility, strength, and mental clarity. Tai chi, a form of martial arts, emphasizes slow, deliberate movements and focused attention, making it a moving meditation. Incorporating mindful movement into your exercise routines can enhance physical and mental health.

Personal stories of transformation through mindful movement are inspiring. Take, for example, a friend of mine who struggled with chronic stress and anxiety. She began incorporating yoga into her daily routine, focusing on breathing and movement. Over time, she noticed a significant reduction in her anxiety levels and an improvement in her overall mood. Another example is a colleague practicing tai chi to manage work-related stress. The slow, rhythmic movements helped her stay present and calm, even during high-pressure situations. These stories highlight the transformative power of mindful movement in everyday life.

Practice Exercise: Walking Meditation

Find a quiet place where you can walk back and forth without distractions. Stand still momentarily, taking a few deep breaths to center yourself. As you start walking, focus on the sensations of each step. Feel your feet touching the ground, notice the movement of your legs, and pay attention to the rhythm of your gait. Try to synchronize your breath with your steps, inhaling for four steps and exhaling for four. Continue walking mindfully for five to ten minutes, observing any changes in your mind and body. This practice can be easily integrated into your daily routine, offering peace and grounding amidst your busy schedule.

Mindful Eating Practices

Mindful eating is a practice that goes beyond simply nourishing your body. It's about engaging all your senses and being fully present during your meals. Mindful eating means paying close attention to the experience of eating without judgment. It involves savoring each bite, noticing your food's colors, textures, and flavors, and truly appreciating the act of eating. By doing so, you not only enhance your dining experience but also improve your digestion and satisfaction levels. Eating mindfully allows your body to signal hunger and fullness cues more effectively, helping you avoid overeating and promoting better digestion.

The principles of mindful eating are rooted in mindfulness, which means focusing on the present moment. This can significantly impact your relationship with food. For instance, when you eat mindlessly, you might eat quickly, barely taste your food, or eat while distracted by TV or work. In contrast, mindful eating encourages you to slow down and appreciate each bite. This can lead to greater satisfaction and enjoyment, making your meals more fulfilling both physically and emotionally.

Mindful eating also offers psychological benefits. It can help reduce stress and anxiety around food, making mealtime a more relaxing and enjoyable experience. By being present and fully engaged with your food, you can cultivate a healthier relationship with eating, free from guilt or anxiety. This practice can also help you become more attuned to your body's needs, allowing you to make more conscious and nourishing food choices.

Practicing mindful eating involves a few simple techniques. Start by eating slowly and savoring each bite. Take the time to chew your food thoroughly, noticing its texture and flavor. This not only enhances your eating experience but also aids digestion. Pay attention to the colors, textures, and tastes of your food. Notice the vibrant colors of vegetables, the smooth texture of yogurt, or the crunch of a fresh apple. Engaging your senses in this way can make each meal a more immersive and enjoyable experience.

Listening to your body's hunger and fullness cues is another crucial aspect of mindful eating. Before you start eating, take a moment to check in with your body. Are you truly hungry or eating out of habit or emotion? Throughout the meal, pause occasionally to assess your level of fullness. This can help you avoid overeating and make more conscious food choices. By tuning into your body's signals, you can eat in a way that truly nourishes you rather than simply filling a void.

Emotional eating is a common challenge that many of us face. We often use food for comfort during stress, sadness, or boredom. Mindful eating can help address these emotional eating habits by encouraging you to identify your emotional triggers for eating. When you feel the urge to eat, pause and ask yourself if you're truly hungry or trying to soothe an emotion. Practicing self-compassion during emotional eating episodes is essential. Acknowledge your feelings and offer yourself kindness instead of judging yourself for turning to food for comfort. This can help break the cycle of emotional eating and promote a healthier relationship with food.

Techniques for redirecting emotional eating behaviors include finding alternative ways to cope with your emotions. Instead of reaching for a snack when stressed, try taking a walk, practicing deep breathing, or calling a friend. These activities can provide the comfort and distraction you seek without the negative consequences of emotional eating. Over time, you can develop healthier coping mechanisms that support your overall well-being.

Integrating mindful eating into your daily life doesn't have to be complicated. Start by creating a calm and distraction-free eating environment. Turn off the TV, put away your phone, and focus solely on your meal. This can help you fully engage with your food and enjoy the experience. Setting intentions before meals can also be beneficial. Take a moment to express gratitude for your food and set an intention for mindful eating. This simple practice can help you approach your meals with mindfulness and appreciation.

Practicing gratitude for food and its sources is another powerful way to enhance your mindful eating practice. Before you begin eating, take a moment to reflect on the journey your food has taken to reach your plate. Consider the farmers who grew the produce, the workers who transported it, and the chefs who prepared it. This practice can deepen your appreciation for your food and make each meal a more meaningful experience.

Mindful eating is a powerful practice that can transform your relationship with food. Being fully present and engaged during meals can improve your digestion, reduce stress, and cultivate a healthier relationship with eating. As you incorporate these techniques into your daily life, mindful eating becomes a natural and enjoyable part of your routine.

Next, we'll explore how mindfulness techniques can help you manage anxiety and emotional regulation. These practices will provide you with tools to navigate life's challenges with greater ease and resilience.

FOUR

Managing Anxiety Through Mindfulness

I remember sitting in a crowded café, trying to enjoy a cup of coffee, when a sudden wave of anxiety hit me out of nowhere. My heart started racing, and my palms got sweaty. All I wanted was to bolt out of there. It was baffling because there was no apparent reason for my anxiety. This experience made me realize how crucial it is to understand what triggers these anxious episodes. Identifying these triggers is often the first step in managing anxiety effectively.

Identifying Anxiety Triggers

Anxiety triggers are specific events, situations, or even thoughts that cause your anxiety to spike. Understanding these triggers is like finding the key to a locked door. Once you identify them, you can manage and reduce their impact on your life. Common types of anxiety triggers include social situations, work stress, and even memories from past experiences. For instance, you might feel a rush of anxiety before giving a presentation at work or when you're in a crowded room. Sometimes, the trigger isn't as obvious—it could be a specific sound, smell, or even a fleeting thought that brings back a stressful memory. Past experiences, especially traumatic ones, can play a significant role in current anxiety. These experiences get stored in your brain and can resurface as anxiety triggers, even if you don't consciously remember them.

Becoming self-aware is crucial in identifying these triggers. One effective technique is journaling. Try keeping a journal to track your anxiety episodes. Whenever you feel anxious, jot down the details of the situation: where you were, what you were doing, and what thoughts were running through your mind. Over time, you may notice patterns. For example, you might realize that your anxiety spikes every Monday morning before work or whenever you have to attend a social gathering. This awareness can be incredibly empowering, as it gives you insight into what specifically triggers your anxiety.

Mindfulness meditation is another powerful tool for self-awareness. Set aside a few minutes daily to sit quietly and observe your thoughts and feelings without judgment. This practice can help you become more attuned to the subtle cues that indicate an anxiety trigger is present. For instance, you might notice a tightening in your chest or a racing heart whenever you think about an upcoming event. This heightened awareness can help you identify triggers you might not have been conscious of before. Daily reflection practices, like taking a few moments before bed to review your day, can also help you pinpoint what triggered your anxiety and how you responded to it.

Once you've started to identify your anxiety triggers, the next step is to analyze patterns. Keeping an anxiety log can be incredibly helpful for this. In your log, note down each anxiety episode along with the details of the situation. After a few weeks, review your log to identify any recurring themes or situations. You might notice that certain people, places, or activities consistently trigger your anxiety. For example, work-related stress is a significant trigger. Identifying these patterns can help you take proactive steps to manage your anxiety more effectively.

It is also essential to use mindfulness to notice subtle triggers. Sometimes, the triggers are not obvious and can be as subtle as a particular scent or a specific type of lighting. Mindfulness can help you become more aware of these subtle cues. For instance, you might realize that a particular perfume reminds you of a stressful event from your past, triggering anxiety. This awareness allows you to address the root cause of your anxiety rather than just its symptoms.

Practical Exercise: Guided Self-Reflection Questions

Take a moment to sit quietly with a journal and reflect on the following questions:

1. When was the last time you felt a sudden rush of anxiety? What were you doing at that moment?
2. Are there specific situations or people that consistently make you feel anxious?
3. Can you recall any past experiences that might be linked to your current anxiety triggers?
4. How does your body react when you're anxious? Do you notice any specific physical sensations?
5. What thoughts run through your mind when you feel anxious? Are there any common themes?

Write down your answers and review them periodically to identify patterns and gain deeper insights into your anxiety triggers.

Mindfulness-based stress reduction (MBSR) exercises can also be beneficial. These exercises help you better understand your thoughts, feelings, and bodily sensations. One effective MBSR exercise is the body scan, where you systematically focus your attention on different parts of your body, noticing any tension or discomfort. This practice can help you become more aware of the physical sensations associated with anxiety, making it easier to identify triggers.

Cognitive-behavioral techniques (CBT) are another valuable tool for identifying anxiety triggers. CBT involves examining the thoughts and beliefs that contribute to your anxiety and challenging them. For instance, if you notice that you feel anxious whenever you think about a particular task at work, you can use CBT techniques to explore and challenge the underlying beliefs that contribute to this anxiety. By identifying and addressing these cognitive patterns, you can reduce the impact of anxiety triggers on your life.

Understanding your anxiety triggers is a vital step in managing anxiety. By becoming more self-aware and analyzing patterns, you can gain valuable insights into what specifically triggers your anxiety. This knowledge empowers you to take proactive steps to manage and reduce anxiety, leading to greater inner peace and well-being.

Mindful Breathing for Anxiety Relief

Mindful breathing is a lifeline in moments of anxiety. Focusing on your breath can bring immediate calm when your heart races and thoughts spiral. It works by activating the parasympathetic nervous system, which counteracts the fight-or-flight response. This shift helps to slow your heart rate, reduce blood pressure, and relax your muscles. The beauty of mindful breathing lies in its simplicity. No matter where you are, you can turn to your breath for relief. I remember a particularly stressful day when I felt overwhelmed by work deadlines. I stepped outside, closed my eyes, and focused on my breath. Within minutes, I felt a wave of calm wash over me, allowing me to return to my tasks with a clearer mind.

Advanced breathing techniques can take your practice to the next level. One such technique is the three-part breath or Dirga

Pranayama. This involves breathing deeply into three parts of your abdomen: first, the lower belly, then the ribcage, and finally, the upper chest. Start by placing one hand on your belly and the other on your chest. Inhale deeply, feel your belly rise, your ribcage expands, and your chest lift. Exhale slowly in reverse order. This technique helps to maximize lung capacity and brings a profound sense of relaxation.

Another powerful technique is the ocean breath, or Ujjayi Pranayama, often used in yoga. To practice, inhale deeply through your nose, then exhale while slightly constricting the back of your throat. This creates a soft, ocean-like sound. The rhythmic nature of this breath can be incredibly soothing, making it an excellent choice for moments of high anxiety.

Resonant or coherent breathing involves inhaling and exhaling for equal lengths, typically around six seconds each. This technique helps to synchronize your breath with your heart rate, promoting a state of calm and balance. It's particularly useful for reducing anxiety and improving overall heart health.

Guided breathing exercises tailored for anxiety relief can be incredibly effective. One approach is to combine breathing with guided imagery. Close your eyes and imagine a peaceful place, like a beach or a forest. As you breathe in, visualize the scenery, and as you breathe out, imagine releasing your anxiety. Another method is to use your breath as an anchor during anxious moments. When you feel anxiety rising, focus solely on your breath. Count each inhale and exhale, aiming for a steady, rhythmic pattern. This can ground you and bring you back to the present moment.

Breath counting is another simple yet powerful exercise for managing anxiety. Sit comfortably and close your eyes. Begin by taking a deep breath in and then slowly exhaling. On the next inhale, silently count "one." On the next exhale, count "two." Continue this pattern up to the count of ten, then start over. This technique can help to focus your mind and reduce anxious thoughts.

Integrating these breathing practices into your daily life can make a significant difference. During high-stress times, take a few minutes to practice mindful breathing. Whether you're in the middle of a hectic workday or dealing with a challenging situation at home, focusing on your breath can provide immediate relief. Incorporating breathing exercises into your morning routine can set a positive tone for the day. Start your morning with a few minutes of deep, mindful breathing to center yourself before diving into your tasks. This can help to reduce stress and improve your focus throughout the day.

Using mindful breathing before social engagements can also be beneficial. If you often feel anxious in social situations, take a few moments to focus on your breath before entering the event. This can help to calm your nerves and make the experience more enjoyable. Practicing mindful breathing regularly can create a sense of inner peace and resilience, making it easier to navigate life's challenges.

Mindful breathing is a simple yet powerful tool for managing anxiety. By incorporating these advanced techniques and guided exercises into your daily routine, you can create moments of calm and clarity, deepening your sense of inner peace.

Grounding Techniques to Stay Present

Grounding techniques are invaluable when it comes to managing anxiety. They are methods that help you stay anchored in the present moment, pulling you out of your anxious thoughts and bringing you back to reality. Think of grounding as a way to tether yourself to the here and now, which can be incredibly calming when anxiety threatens to pull you away. Grounding helps manage anxiety by shifting your focus from the overwhelming feelings in your mind to the tangible sensations in your body. This connection between grounding and mindfulness is important. Both practices encourage you to be present, but grounding is particularly effective in acute anxiety.

Sensory grounding techniques engage your senses—sight, sound, touch, taste, and smell—to bring your mind back to the present. The 5-4-3-2-1 technique is a great place to start. Look around and identify five things you can see, four things you can touch, three things you can hear, two things you can smell, and one thing you can taste. This method can help divert your attention from anxious thoughts to the immediate environment. Touch objects like stress balls or textured items can also be very grounding. The physical sensation of squeezing a stress ball or running your fingers over a textured item can help you focus on something other than your anxiety. Aromatherapy is another effective sensory grounding technique. Scents like lavender, chamomile, or sandalwood can be incredibly soothing. You might find it helpful to carry a small vial of essential oil with you for moments when you need to ground yourself quickly.

Cognitive grounding techniques involve using mental exercises to stay present. Counting backward from 100 is a simple yet effective method. The concentration required to count backward can help distract you from anxious thoughts. Reciting a favorite poem or song lyrics can also be a mental anchor. Familiarity with the words can provide comfort and stability. Mental visualization of a calming place is another powerful cognitive grounding technique. Close your eyes and imagine a place where you feel completely at peace. It could be a beach, a forest, or even a cozy room in your house. Visualize every detail, from the colors and textures to the sounds and smells. This mental escape can provide a much-needed break from anxiety.

Physical grounding techniques involve movement or physical sensations to bring you back to the present. Walking barefoot is a simple yet effective way to ground yourself. Your feet touching the ground can help you feel more connected to your environment.

Progressive muscle relaxation is another excellent physical grounding technique. Start by tensing and then relaxing each muscle group in your body, beginning with your toes and working your way up to your head. This practice can help release physical tension and promote relaxation. Physical exercise with mindful attention, such as yoga or tai chi, can also be incredibly grounding. These practices combine movement with mindfulness, helping you stay present while also benefiting your physical health.

Grounding techniques are versatile and can be adapted to fit into your daily routine. Whether you're at home, at work, or out and about, you can use these methods to manage anxiety and stay present. The key is to find the techniques that work best for you and practice them regularly. Over time, grounding can become a natural and effective way to manage anxiety and maintain a sense of inner peace.

Creating a Calm Space

Your environment plays a significant role in how you feel. Walking into a cluttered room makes it easy to feel overwhelmed and stressed. Clutter can be a constant visual reminder of chaos, making relaxing and finding peace difficult. On the other hand, a calm and organized space can have the opposite effect. It can create a sense of order and tranquility, making it easier to manage anxiety and stress. Imagine walking into a tidy room with soft lighting, soothing colors, and a few well-placed plants. The difference is palpable. Your mind feels at ease, allowing you to breathe a little easier.

Designing a calming space can be done without a complete home makeover. Start with small, intentional changes. Choose soothing colors for your walls and décor. Soft blues, greens, and neutral tones can create a peaceful atmosphere. Avoid bright or harsh colors that can be overstimulating. Incorporating natural elements can also enhance the calming effect. Plants, water features, and natural light can bring a sense of life and serenity to your space. Even a small potted plant on your desk or a water fountain in the corner can make a big difference. Creating dedicated mindfulness areas is another effective strategy. Set aside a corner of your home or office where you can practice mindfulness or simply relax. This could be a cozy chair with a soft blanket, a yoga mat, or even a small altar with items that bring peace.

Mindful organization is about more than just tidying up; it's about creating a space that supports your well-being. Start by decluttering your space. Go through your belongings and decide what you truly need and can let go of. This process can be incredibly liberating. Mindful cleaning practices can also help you maintain a calm space. Instead of rushing through chores, take your time and focus on each task. Notice the smell of the cleaning products, the feel of the cloth in your hand, and the satisfaction of seeing a clean surface. Organizing with intention means placing items in a way that makes sense to you and supports your daily routine. For example, keep your most-used items within easy reach and store less frequently used items out of sight.

Maintaining a calm space requires regular attention. Establishing mindful tidying routines can help you keep your space organized over time. Spend a few minutes daily tidying up rather than letting things pile up. This can prevent clutter from becoming overwhelming. Seasonal reorganization practices can also be helpful. Take some time at the beginning of each season to reassess your space and make any necessary changes. This could include swapping out seasonal décor, reorganizing storage, or deep cleaning certain areas. Setting boundaries to protect your calm space is crucial. Make it clear to others that this space is important for your well-being and should be respected. Whether it's a no-clutter rule or designated quiet times, these boundaries can help maintain the sanctuary you've created.

By creating a calm space, you can significantly reduce your anxiety levels and promote a sense of inner peace. The environment you surround yourself with can either contribute to your stress or help alleviate it. You can create a sanctuary that supports your emotional well-being by making intentional choices and maintaining a mindful organization. This calm space can serve as a refuge from the chaos of daily life, providing a place where you can relax, recharge, and practice mindfulness.

FIVE

Emotional Awareness and Regulation

I remember a particular day when I was overwhelmed with emotions. I had just received some unexpected news at work, and it felt like the ground had been pulled out from under me. My heart raced, my hands trembled, and I couldn't focus on anything else. Later that evening, as I sat quietly reflecting on the day, I realized that an old memory of a similar situation triggered my intense reaction. This moment was a revelation—it made me understand the power of emotional triggers and how they can affect our responses.

Understanding Emotional Triggers

Emotional triggers are specific experiences, memories, or events that spark intense emotional reactions. These reactions can be overwhelming and often seem disproportionate to the situation. For example, a casual comment from a coworker might trigger feelings of rejection, or a particular scent might bring back a flood of memories from a painful period. These triggers are deeply personal and can vary widely from one person to another. Common sources of emotional triggers include past experiences, relationships, and even unconscious biases that we've developed over time.

Past experiences play a significant role in shaping our emotional triggers. For instance, if you experienced betrayal in a past relationship, you might feel anxious or distrustful in new relationships, even when there's no immediate reason for concern. Past and present relationships are also fertile ground for emotional triggers. A critical comment from a partner or a perceived slight from a friend can bring up deep-seated feelings of inadequacy or rejection. Unconscious biases can trigger emotional responses, too. These biases often form in childhood and can affect how we perceive and react to certain situations.

Reflecting on your emotional triggers is the first step toward understanding and managing them. Journaling can be an incredibly effective tool for this. Set aside time each day to write about your experiences and emotions. When did you feel particularly upset or anxious? What was happening at that moment? By regularly journaling, you can identify patterns and pinpoint specific triggers. Mindful reflection exercises can also be beneficial. Take a few minutes each day to sit quietly and reflect on your emotional responses. What thoughts and feelings arise when you think about certain situations or people? This practice can help you become more aware of your triggers and how they affect you.

Identifying patterns in your emotional responses is crucial. Over time, certain situations consistently trigger strong reactions. For example, you might feel particularly anxious during work team meetings or become defensive whenever someone criticizes your work. Recognizing these patterns can help you anticipate and manage your triggers more effectively.

Emotional triggers can have a profound impact on our behavior and decision-making. When triggered, we might react in ways that are out of character or that we later regret. For example, you might avoid social situations because they trigger insecurity or lash out in anger when you feel disrespected. These behaviors are often automatic responses to the underlying emotional trigger. The connection between triggers and stress responses is well-documented. When triggered, our bodies become heightened alert, activating the fight-or-flight response. This can lead to physical symptoms like a pounding heart, sweaty palms, or an upset stomach.

Managing Emotional Triggers

Case studies can illustrate the impact of emotional triggers. Take Allie, for example. She experienced intense anxiety whenever she received feedback at work. Through journaling and therapy, she realized that this anxiety was linked to her childhood experiences of being harshly criticized by a parent. By understanding this connection, Allie was able to develop healthier coping mechanisms and reduce her anxiety during feedback sessions.

Managing emotional triggers involves both short-term and long-term strategies. Mindfulness techniques can be incredibly effective for early detection of triggers. When you notice a strong emotional response, take a moment to pause and breathe. Use mindful breathing to ground yourself and create a space between the trigger and your reaction. Developing healthy coping mechanisms is also crucial. This might involve talking to a trusted friend, practicing self-compassion, or engaging in activities that help you relax and recharge.

Creating a trigger action plan can provide a structured approach to managing your triggers. Start by identifying your most common triggers and the situations in which they occur. Next, outline specific strategies for managing these triggers when they arise. For example, if social situations trigger anxiety, your action plan might include practicing deep breathing exercises before attending an event and setting a time limit for how long you'll stay. Having a plan can help you feel more prepared and in control.

Reflection Exercise: Exploring Emotional Triggers

Take a few moments to reflect on your emotional triggers. Consider the following questions and write down your thoughts:

1. What situations or experiences consistently evoke strong emotional reactions in you?
2. Can you trace these reactions back to past experiences or relationships?
3. How do these emotional triggers affect your behavior and decision-making?
4. What physical symptoms do you notice when you're triggered?
5. What strategies have you found helpful in managing your emotional triggers?

Understanding and managing your emotional triggers allows you to navigate life's challenges with greater ease and resilience. This awareness allows you to respond to situations thoughtfully rather than impulsively, creating a deeper sense of inner peace and emotional balance.

Mindful Observation of Emotions

The Practice of Observing Emotions means tuning into your feelings without trying to change or judge them. It's about noticing the waves of emotion that pass through you, allowing them to exist without immediately reacting. Observing emotions mindfully involves separating the emotion from your reaction to it. For example, if you feel anger rising, instead of lashing out or suppressing it, you simply acknowledge its presence. This practice can be incredibly liberating. It allows you to understand your emotional landscape better and respond more thoughtfully. The benefits are numerous. Mindful observation can reduce the intensity of negative emotions, improve emotional regulation, and create a sense of inner peace.

To practice mindful observation, start with a body scan to notice emotional sensations. Find a quiet place to sit or lie down, close your eyes, and take a few deep breaths. Begin by focusing on your toes and slowly move your attention up through your body, noticing any areas of tension or discomfort. As you do this, pay attention to any emotional sensations that arise. For instance, you might notice a tightness in your chest that corresponds with anxiety or a heaviness in your shoulders that signals stress. This body scan can help you become more aware of the physical manifestations of your emotions.

Another effective technique is labeling your emotions without judgment. When you notice an emotion, simply give it a name. "This is anger," or "This is sadness." By labeling the emotion, you create a space between yourself and the feeling, which can make it less overwhelming. It's like stepping back and observing a storm from a safe distance rather than being caught in the middle. This practice can help you understand your emotions better and respond more calmly.

Using your breath as an anchor during emotional waves is another powerful tool. When you feel a strong emotion coming on, focus on your breath. Take slow, deep breaths, and pay attention to the sensation of air entering and leaving your body. This can help ground you and keep you present, preventing the emotion from taking over. Imagine your breath as a steady anchor that holds you in place while the emotional storm passes. This technique can be particularly useful in moments of intense emotion, providing a simple yet effective way to stay centered.

Staying present with difficult emotions without becoming overwhelmed is a skill that takes practice. One technique is grounding yourself during intense emotions. This can involve focusing on your senses to return to the present moment. For example, you might press your feet firmly into the ground, hold a textured object, or focus on the sounds around you. These grounding techniques can help you stay present and prevent the emotion from spiraling out of control.

Practicing self-compassion during emotional observation is also crucial. When you notice a difficult emotion, offer yourself kindness and understanding. Remind yourself that it's okay to feel this way and that it's a natural part of being human. This self-compassion can create a sense of safety and support, making staying present with the emotion easier. Recognizing the transient nature of emotions can also be incredibly helpful. Emotions are like waves—they rise, peak, and eventually fade. Remind yourself that this difficult emotion, too, will pass. This awareness can make the emotion feel less permanent and more manageable.

Reflective practices can deepen your emotional awareness. A daily emotion log is a great way to track your emotional experiences. Each day, take a few minutes to write down your emotions, what triggered them, and how you responded. This practice can help you identify patterns and gain deeper insights into your emotional landscape. Guided mindful journaling exercises can also be beneficial. Set aside time each day to journal about your emotions, using prompts to guide your reflection. For example, you might write about a recent emotional experience and explore how you felt, what triggered it, and how you responded. This reflective practice can help you understand your emotions better and develop healthier ways to manage them.

Personal stories of transformation through mindful observation can be inspiring. Take Emily, for example. She struggled with intense bouts of anger that would often lead to arguments with her partner. Through mindful observation, she learned to notice the early signs of anger, such as a tightening in her chest and rapid breathing. Labeling the emotion and using her breath as an anchor, she could stay present and choose a more thoughtful response. This practice transformed her relationship, reducing conflicts and creating a deeper connection.

Mindful observation of emotions is a powerful practice that can help you better understand and manage your emotional landscape. By observing your emotions mindfully, you can create a sense of inner peace and emotional balance. This practice allows you to respond to emotions thoughtfully rather than reacting impulsively, leading to healthier and more fulfilling relationships.

Techniques for Emotional Regulation

Emotional regulation is the ability to manage and respond to emotional experiences healthily. It's not about suppressing your emotions or pretending they don't exist. Instead, it's about understanding your emotions, accepting them, and finding constructive ways to cope with them. This skill is crucial for mental well-being because it helps you navigate life's ups and downs without becoming overwhelmed. When you can regulate your emotions, you're better equipped to handle stress, maintain healthy relationships, and make thoughtful decisions.

One common misconception is that emotional regulation means pushing your emotions aside. This couldn't be further from the truth. Suppression involves ignoring or denying your feelings, which can lead to increased stress and emotional outbursts later on. Emotional regulation, on the other hand, involves acknowledging your emotions and dealing with them in a healthy and constructive way. For instance, if you feel angry, instead of bottling it up, you might take a few deep breaths, acknowledge your anger, and find a healthy outlet for it, like talking to a friend or walking.

The role of emotional regulation in stress management cannot be overstated. When you can regulate your emotions, you're less likely to feel overwhelmed by stress. You can approach stressful situations with a clear mind and a calm demeanor, making it easier to find solutions and navigate challenges. This skill is particularly important for managing anxiety and perfectionism, as it helps you maintain balance and perspective.

Mindfulness-based techniques are incredibly effective for emotional regulation. One popular method is the RAIN technique, which stands for Recognize, Allow, Investigate, and Nurture. When you experience a strong emotion, start by recognizing it. Name the emotion and acknowledge its presence. Next, allow the emotion to be there without trying to change it. Investigate the emotion with curiosity, exploring its origins and how it feels in your body. Finally, nurture yourself with kindness and compassion, offering yourself the understanding and support you need.

Another useful practice is the S.T.O.P. technique: Stop, Take a breath, Observe, Proceed. When you feel overwhelmed, pause and take a deep breath. Observe what's happening inside you and around you. What thoughts are running through your mind? What physical sensations are you experiencing? Then, proceed with a mindful response instead of a knee-jerk reaction. This simple technique can create a space between your emotion and reaction, allowing you to choose a more thoughtful response.

The emotion surfboard method is another valuable tool. Imagine your emotions as waves in the ocean. Some waves are small and gentle, while others are large and powerful. Instead of fighting the waves or getting swept away, picture yourself riding them on a surfboard. Stay balanced and ride each wave as it comes, knowing it will eventually pass. This visualization can help you remain steady and calm amidst emotional turbulence.

Cognitive-behavioral approaches complement mindfulness practices and offer additional tools for emotional regulation. Cognitive restructuring, for example, involves identifying and challenging negative thought patterns. When you notice a negative thought, ask yourself if it's based on facts or assumptions. Then, reframe the thought in a more balanced and realistic way. This can help shift your perspective and reduce the emotional impact of negative thinking.

Thought-stopping techniques are also effective. When contemplating or spiraling into negative thoughts, use a mental cue to interrupt the pattern. You might say "stop" to yourself or visualize a stop sign. Then, redirect your focus to something positive or neutral. This practice can help break the cycle of negative thinking and prevent it from escalating.

Reframing negative thoughts is another powerful strategy. Instead of seeing a situation as entirely negative, look for the silver lining or a different perspective. For example, if you make a mistake at work, instead of beating yourself up, consider what you can learn from the experience. This shift in perspective can reduce the emotional weight of negative experiences and promote a more positive outlook.

Creating an emotional regulation plan can provide a structured approach to managing emotions. Start by identifying your triggers and typical responses. What situations or experiences tend to evoke strong emotions? How do you usually react? Once you clearly understand your triggers and responses, develop a step-by-step regulation strategy. This might include mindfulness practices, cognitive-behavioral techniques, and healthy coping mechanisms. Incorporate these practices into your daily routine to build emotional resilience and improve your ability to regulate emotions.

By understanding and employing these techniques, you can develop a robust emotional regulation plan that supports your mental well-being. Emotional regulation is a skill that can be cultivated with practice and patience, leading to a deeper sense of inner peace and balance.

Building Emotional Resilience

Emotional resilience is the ability to bounce back from life's challenges and setbacks. It's about maintaining a stable emotional state even when things go wrong. Emotional resilience isn't about never experiencing negative emotions but rather about how quickly and effectively you can recover from them. The benefits of emotional resilience are profound. Resilient individuals tend to have better mental health, stronger relationships, and greater overall well-being. They are more adaptable, can handle stress better, and are often more optimistic about the future.

Imagine a storm hitting a tree. A resilient tree bends with the wind but doesn't break. Similarly, resilient individuals can endure stress and adversity without crumbling. They find ways to cope, adapt, and eventually thrive even in the face of challenges. This resilience is closely linked to overall well-being because it enables you to navigate life's ups and downs with balance and stability. Examples of resilient behaviors include seeking support when needed, maintaining a positive outlook, and using setbacks as opportunities for growth.

Mindfulness practices can play a crucial role in building emotional resilience. Loving-kindness meditation is one such practice. This involves directing feelings of love and compassion towards yourself and others. By regularly practicing loving-kindness meditation, you can cultivate a sense of warmth and connection, which can bolster your emotional resilience. Gratitude journaling is another powerful tool. Each day, take a few minutes to write down things you're grateful for. This practice can shift your focus from what's going wrong to what's going right, fostering a more positive outlook and enhancing resilience.

Mindful self-reflection is also essential. Set aside time each day to reflect on your experiences and emotions. This can help you gain insights into your emotional responses and develop healthier coping methods. Regularly engaging in mindful self-reflection can build a deeper understanding of yourself and strengthen your emotional resilience.

Cultivating a growth mindset is another key factor in developing emotional resilience. A growth mindset is the belief that you can develop your abilities and intelligence through effort and learning. This contrasts with a fixed mindset, which holds that your abilities are static and unchangeable. By adopting a growth mindset, you can view challenges as opportunities for growth rather than threats. Techniques for fostering a growth mindset include embracing challenges, learning from criticism, and persisting in the face of setbacks.

Case studies illustrate the power of a growth mindset in building resilience. Take the example of Amanda, who faced significant setbacks in her career. Instead of viewing these setbacks as failures, she saw them as opportunities to learn and grow. By adopting a growth mindset, Amanda could bounce back stronger, eventually achieving even greater success. Her resilience was about enduring the challenges and using them as stepping stones for personal and professional growth.

Social support is another crucial element in building emotional resilience. Identifying supportive relationships can provide a safety net during tough times. These relationships might include friends, family members, colleagues, or support groups. Techniques for seeking and offering support involve open communication, active listening, and being present for others. Creating a community of resilience means surrounding yourself with people who understand and support your journey.

Building a support network can significantly enhance your resilience. For instance, joining a mindfulness group can provide a sense of community and shared experience. These groups offer a safe space to share your struggles and successes, providing emotional support and practical advice. Similarly, cultivating strong relationships with friends and family can provide comfort and encouragement during difficult times.

Focusing on these practices and principles can help you build emotional resilience and navigate life's challenges with greater ease and confidence. Emotional resilience is not a trait you're born with but a skill you can develop through mindful practices, a growth mindset, and a strong support network. This resilience will be a foundation for your well-being, helping you maintain balance and find peace amidst life's inevitable storms.

Next, we'll explore how to integrate mindfulness into everyday activities, making it a seamless part of your life. This will help you maintain the emotional resilience you've built and continue to grow in your journey toward inner peace.

SIX

Overcoming Negative Self-Talk

One day, I was getting ready for a big presentation at work. I stood in front of the mirror, rehearsing my lines, but all I could hear was that nagging voice in my head saying, "You're going to mess this up. Everyone will see how incompetent you are." My chest tightened, and I felt a wave of panic. It was at that moment I realized how powerful negative self-talk could be and how it had been undermining my confidence for years. I knew it was time to address these harmful thoughts head-on.

Recognizing Negative Thought Patterns

Negative self-talk refers to the critical, negative, or punishing internal comments about ourselves. These thoughts can be incredibly damaging, influencing our mental health and self-image. When you constantly hear a voice in your head telling you that you're not good enough, it's hard not to believe it. This internal dialogue can keep you stuck in a cycle of self-doubt and anxiety, making it challenging to move forward and achieve your goals.

Negative self-talk comes in various forms. One common type is catastrophizing, where you imagine the worst possible outcome in any situation. For instance, if you make a small mistake at work, you might think, "I'm going to get fired for this." Another type is overgeneralizing, where you see a single negative event as a never-ending pattern of defeat. For example, if you fail a test, you might think, "I always fail at everything." These thoughts can erode your self-esteem and mental well-being, leaving you feeling hopeless and defeated.

The impact of negative self-talk on self-esteem and mental well-being is profound. Constantly berating yourself can lead to feelings of worthlessness and depression. It can also increase your anxiety, as you're always anticipating failure or rejection. Over time, this negative internal dialogue can become a self-fulfilling prophecy. When you believe you're not good enough, you may stop trying, reinforcing the very failures you fear.

Common negative thought patterns include all-or-nothing thinking, where you see things in black-and-white terms. If something isn't perfect, it's a complete failure. Mental filtering is another pattern where you focus on the negative aspects of a situation and ignore the positive. For example, you might receive a glowing performance review but fixate on one constructive criticism. Disqualifying the positive involves rejecting positive experiences by insisting they "don't count." You might think, "Sure, I got a promotion, but it's just because no one else wanted the job." Jumping to conclusions is another pattern, where you make negative assumptions without evidence. For instance, you might assume someone is mad at you even though they haven't said anything to suggest that.

Self-monitoring techniques can help you become aware of your negative thought patterns. Keeping a thought diary is an effective method. Write down your thoughts throughout the day, especially when you notice a shift in your mood. Note what you were doing and how you felt. This can help you identify recurring patterns and specific triggers for your negative self-talk. Mindfulness meditation is another powerful tool. Practicing mindfulness lets you observe your thoughts without getting caught up in them. This awareness can help you recognize negative self-talk as it happens, allowing you to challenge and change it.

Using phone apps to track negative thoughts can also be helpful. Apps like Thought Diary or CBT Thought Record Diary can assist you in recording and analyzing your thoughts. These apps often include prompts and exercises to help you reframe negative thoughts and develop a more balanced perspective. The convenience of having these tools on your phone makes it easier to integrate self-monitoring into your daily routine.

Understanding the triggers for your negative self-talk is crucial. Reflecting on past experiences can provide valuable insights. Think about situations where you felt particularly down on yourself. What was happening at the time? Were you under a lot of stress? Did someone say something that made you doubt yourself? Identifying specific triggers, such as stressful work situations or social interactions, can help you anticipate and manage your negative self-talk.

Using mindfulness to notice immediate reactions can also be beneficial. Pay attention to how your body feels when you're experiencing negative self-talk. Do you feel tension in your shoulders? Is your heart racing? These physical sensations can serve as cues to check in with your thoughts. When you notice these reactions, take a moment to breathe deeply and observe your thoughts without judgment. This can help you interrupt the cycle of negative self-talk and create space for more positive, constructive thoughts.

Reflection Exercise: Identifying Negative Thought Patterns

Take a moment to reflect on your recent thoughts. Write down any negative thoughts you've had in the past week. Note the context and how you felt at the time. Look for patterns and triggers. Are there specific situations that tend to bring out your negative self-talk? How do these thoughts impact your mood and behavior? This exercise can help you become more aware of your thought patterns and provide a starting point for changing them.

Recognizing and understanding your negative thought patterns is the first step towards overcoming them. By becoming aware of these patterns and their triggers, you can start challenging and changing your negative self-talk, paving the way for a more positive and balanced mindset.

Transforming Negative Thoughts

Cognitive restructuring is a powerful method to challenge and change negative thought patterns. This therapeutic technique involves deconstructing unhelpful thoughts and rebuilding them in a balanced and accurate way. Imagine you're wearing a pair of dark glasses that distort your vision; cognitive restructuring helps you swap those for clearer lenses. The process begins with identifying a negative thought. Once pinpointing the thought, ask yourself if it's based on facts or assumptions. Often, our negative thoughts are not grounded in reality. Next, challenge the thought by considering alternative perspectives. For example, if you think, "I always mess up," ask yourself if that's entirely true. Have there been times when you succeeded? Finally, replace the negative thought with a more balanced one, like, "I've made mistakes, but I've also had successes."

Positive reframing is another effective technique for transforming negative thoughts into positive or neutral ones. This involves shifting your perspective to see the situation in a different light. For instance, if you're thinking, "I failed at this project," you can reframe it to, "This project didn't go as planned, but it's an opportunity to learn and improve." Techniques for positive reframing include asking yourself what you can learn from the experience, how you might grow from it, and how you would advise a friend in the same situation. Real-life scenarios show the power of positive reframing. Take Sarah, who was upset about a job rejection. Instead of dwelling on the rejection, she reframed it as a chance to find a better fit for her skills and values. This shift in perspective helped her stay motivated and eventually land a job that was a perfect match.

Mindful self-compassion techniques can also counteract negative self-talk. Loving-kindness meditation focused on self is a powerful practice. Sit comfortably, close your eyes, and bring a sense of warmth and compassion to your mind. Repeat phrases like, "May I be happy. May I be healthy. May I be safe. May I live with ease." This practice helps cultivate a sense of kindness towards yourself, reducing the harshness of negative self-talk. Self-compassion breaks are another useful tool. When you notice negative self-talk, pause and acknowledge it. Say to yourself, "This is a moment of suffering. Suffering is a part of life. May I be kind to myself." This simple practice can shift your mindset from self-criticism to self-compassion, fostering self-acceptance and emotional resilience.

Exercises for fostering self-acceptance can further enhance your ability to counteract negative self-talk. One effective exercise is to write a letter to yourself from the perspective of a compassionate friend. In this letter, acknowledge your struggles and offer words of kindness and encouragement. This practice can help you see yourself through a kinder lens, reducing the impact of negative self-talk. Another exercise is to practice mirror work. Stand before a mirror, look into your eyes, and say kind words to yourself. This can initially feel awkward, but it's a powerful way to build self-acceptance and counteract negative thoughts.

Daily affirmation practice is another powerful tool for replacing negative thoughts with positive ones. Creating personalized affirmations involves identifying areas where you struggle with negative self-talk and crafting positive statements to counteract those thoughts. For example, if you often think, "I'm not good enough," you can create an affirmation like, "I am worthy and capable." Practical tips for daily affirmation practice include writing your affirmations on sticky notes and placing them where you'll see them often, such as on your bathroom mirror or computer screen. You can also set reminders on your phone to repeat your affirmations throughout the day.

Success stories from individuals using affirmations highlight their transformative power. Take Emily, who struggled with self-doubt. She began using affirmations like, "I am confident and strong," and repeated them every morning and evening. Over time, she noticed a shift in her mindset. She felt more confident and less plagued by negative self-talk. Another example is Lisa, who used affirmations to combat feelings of inadequacy at work. By repeating affirmations like, "I am capable and competent," she gradually built her self-esteem and improved her performance.

Transforming negative thoughts takes practice and patience. Cognitive restructuring, positive reframing, mindful self-compassion techniques, and daily affirmations are powerful tools that can help you shift your mindset and cultivate a more positive and balanced outlook.

Affirmations for Self-Love

Imagine waking up each morning to a voice that says, "You are capable, you are strong, and today is your day." This is the power of affirmations. Research supports the effectiveness of affirmations in transforming self-talk. Repeated positive statements can rewire your brain, shifting your mindset from negativity to empowerment. Studies have shown that affirmations can increase neural pathways associated with self-worth and resilience. For example, athletes who use affirmations often perform better because they believe in their abilities. Similarly, individuals who consistently practice positive affirmations report higher self-esteem and mental well-being levels.

Creating effective affirmations requires a bit of thought, but it's well worth the effort. The most powerful affirmations are specific, positive, and in the present tense. Rather than saying, "I will be happy," say, "I am happy." This phrasing helps your mind accept the statement as truth. Personalizing your affirmations is crucial. Think about areas where you struggle with self-love and craft affirmations that speak directly to those issues. For example, if you struggle with feeling worthy, an affirmation like, "I am deserving of love and respect," can be incredibly powerful. Other areas to consider could be confidence, self-acceptance, and resilience. Affirmations like "I trust myself" or "I am enough just as I am" can target these aspects effectively.

Incorporating affirmations into your daily routine can make a significant difference. Start your day with a morning affirmation ritual. As soon as you wake up, take a moment to say your affirmations out loud. This sets a positive tone for the day. Similarly, end your day with evening affirmations to reflect on your accomplishments and reinforce positive self-talk. Using affirmation apps can also be helpful. These apps can send you reminders throughout the day, prompting you to take a moment for positive self-talk. Writing affirmations in visible places is another practical approach. Sticky notes on your mirror, affirmations in your journal, or even setting them as your phone wallpaper can constantly remind you of your worth and capabilities.

Affirmation Exercises: Practicing and Internalizing Affirmations

One effective exercise is affirmation journaling. Write down your affirmations each day and reflect on how they make you feel. Notice any shifts in your mindset or mood. This practice reinforces your positive statements and helps you internalize them. Another powerful exercise is mirror work. Stand in front of a mirror, look into your own eyes, and say your affirmations out loud. This can be challenging at first, but it's incredibly impactful. Looking at yourself while speaking kindness can help break down barriers of self-doubt and build a stronger sense of self-love.

Recording and listening to your affirmations can also be beneficial. Use your phone or a recording device to capture yourself saying your affirmations. Play these recordings during your morning routine, commuting, or before bed. Hearing your voice affirming your worth can amplify the positive impact, making the affirmations feel more genuine and powerful.

Affirmations are not just words; they are powerful tools that can transform your self-talk and boost your self-love. Integrating these practices into your daily life can create a foundation of positivity and resilience, helping you manage anxiety, control, and perfectionism with grace and confidence.

Journaling for Positive Self-Talk

One evening, after a particularly tough day, I found solace in an old notebook. I began writing about my frustrations, my fears, and everything that had been weighing me down. As the pen moved across the paper, something shifted. The chaos in my mind started to clear, and I felt a sense of relief. This was my introduction to the transformative power of journaling.

Journaling offers numerous psychological benefits. Expressive writing helps process emotions, providing a safe space to explore thoughts and feelings. It serves as an emotional release, allowing you to let go of stress and anxiety. Case studies show that individuals who journal regularly experience improved mental clarity and emotional well-being. Take, for instance, Courtney, who struggled with anxiety.

She began journaling daily, and over time, she noticed a significant reduction in her anxiety levels. The act of writing helped her identify triggers and develop healthier coping mechanisms.

There are various journaling techniques specifically aimed at fostering positive self-talk. Gratitude journaling is a powerful practice. Each day, write down three things you're grateful for. This simple act shifts your focus from what's wrong to what's right, fostering a positive mindset. Reflective journaling involves writing about your thoughts and experiences, helping you gain insights and learn from them. This technique encourages self-reflection and growth. Prompt-based journaling is another effective method. You can explore specific aspects of your life and thoughts using guided prompts, facilitating deeper self-awareness and positive self-talk.

Guided journal prompts can help you focus on positive aspects of yourself and your life. Prompts for self-reflection and growth might include questions like, "What have I learned from a recent challenge?" or "How have I grown in the past year?" These questions encourage you to reflect on your progress and achievements. Affirmation-based journal prompts can help reinforce positive self-talk. Write about affirmations you believe in, such as "I am capable of achieving my goals," and reflect on how they make you feel. Prompts for recognizing personal strengths and achievements might include, "What are three things I'm proud of?" or "What strengths have helped me overcome challenges?" These prompts help you acknowledge and celebrate your qualities and accomplishments.

Creating a consistent journaling routine is key to reaping the benefits of this practice. Set aside dedicated journaling time each day. It could be in the morning to set a positive tone for the day or in the evening to reflect on your experiences. Creating a conducive journaling environment can also enhance the experience. Find a quiet, comfortable space where you can write without distractions. Light a candle or play soft music to create a calming atmosphere. Techniques for overcoming writer's block include starting with a simple prompt or free-writing for a few minutes. Remember, there's no right or wrong way to journal. The goal is to express yourself freely and authentically.

Journaling can be a powerful tool for positive self-talk, offering a space to process emotions, reflect on experiences, and celebrate achievements. Integrating journaling into your daily routine can cultivate a positive mindset and enhance your emotional well-being.

In the next chapter, we'll explore practical mindfulness techniques for managing stress and fostering a deeper sense of inner peace.

SEVEN

Balancing Multiple Roles with Mindfulness

I remember a particular morning when I was juggling multiple roles—professional deadlines, family commitments, and personal aspirations. My to-do list felt like a never-ending scroll, and I was drowning in tasks. Then, I realized I needed a different approach to managing my time and responsibilities effectively. This is where mindful time management came into play, transforming my chaotic days into more balanced and fulfilling ones.

Mindful Time Management

Mindfulness can significantly enhance your ability to identify and prioritize tasks effectively. Getting caught up in the whirlwind of daily activities is easy, but mindfulness encourages you to pause and reflect on what truly matters. By paying attention to your life moment by moment, you can make conscious decisions about how to spend your time, committing to what is most important to you. Techniques for mindful prioritization include starting your day with a few minutes of meditation to clear your mind and set your intentions. This practice helps you focus on tasks that align with your values and goals rather than getting sidetracked by less important activities.

Creating a mindful to-do list is another powerful tool. Instead of listing everything you need to do, prioritize tasks by their importance and urgency. Use categories like "Must Do," "Should Do," and "Could Do" to organize your list. This method helps you focus on high-priority tasks first, reducing the overwhelm of a long to-do list. Tools like digital planners or mindfulness apps can assist in creating and managing these lists efficiently. For example, apps like Todoist or Trello allow you to categorize and prioritize tasks, making it easier to stay on track.

Case studies of effective prioritization highlight the benefits of these techniques. Take Mariah, a busy marketing manager and mother of two. By incorporating mindful prioritization into her routine, she could identify and focus on her most important tasks at work and home. She started her day with a brief meditation, listing her top three priorities for the day. This approach helped her stay focused and productive while making time for her family and self-care.

Mindful scheduling is about creating a balanced schedule that allows you to manage your work, family, and personal time effectively. One tip is to block out time for mindfulness practices. Set aside specific times during the day for meditation, deep breathing, or mindful walking. These breaks help you recharge and maintain your focus throughout the day. Examples of balanced daily schedules include a morning routine with meditation, a midday break for a mindful walk, and an evening wind-down with a body scan meditation.

Avoiding over-scheduling is crucial for maintaining balance. It's tempting to fill every minute of your day with tasks, but this can lead to burnout. Instead, leave some buffer time between tasks to allow for unexpected events or simply to take a breather. Strategies for avoiding over-scheduling include setting realistic goals and learning to say no to additional commitments that don't align with your priorities.

Staying present with tasks is essential for reducing stress and increasing productivity. When you focus on one task at a time, you can complete it more efficiently and effectively. Mindful task-switching involves taking a moment to pause and breathe before moving from one task to another. This practice helps you reset and approach each new task with a clear and focused mind. Techniques for minimizing distractions include turning off notifications, setting specific times for checking emails and creating a designated workspace free from interruptions.

Real-life examples of improved focus demonstrate the power of staying present with tasks. Consider Kelsey, a freelance writer struggling to stay focused due to constant distractions. By practicing mindful task-switching and minimizing distractions, she improved her concentration and completed her projects more efficiently. She turned off her phone notifications and set specific times for checking emails, allowing her to stay immersed in her writing.

Reflective time management encourages regular reflection on your time use to make mindful adjustments as needed. Weekly time management reflections help you assess how well you balance your responsibilities and identify areas for improvement. Set aside a few minutes each week to review your schedule and reflect on what worked and what didn't. This practice allows you to make adjustments and realign your priorities.

Journaling prompts for assessing time use can guide your reflections. Questions like "What tasks brought me the most satisfaction this week?" and "Were there any activities that felt like a waste of time?" can help you gain insights into how you spend your time. Techniques for realigning priorities include adjusting your to-do list, setting new goals, and making deliberate choices about where to focus your energy.

By incorporating mindful time management practices into your routine, you can more effectively balance your multiple roles, reduce stress, and create a sense of inner peace.

Setting Boundaries with Mindfulness

Understanding personal boundaries is crucial for mental well-being. Personal boundaries are the limits and rules we set for ourselves within relationships, defining what we are comfortable with and how we wish to be treated. These boundaries can be emotional, physical, or related to time. Emotional boundaries involve protecting your feelings and mental health, ensuring that others do not manipulate or emotionally drain you. Physical boundaries pertain to your personal space and physical touch. Time boundaries involve managing how you spend your time and energy, ensuring you have time for yourself and your priorities. Establishing and maintaining these boundaries can significantly reduce stress and help you manage anxiety and control.

Mindful boundary setting involves being aware of your needs and communicating them clearly and compassionately. Start by identifying what your boundaries are. This requires self-reflection and mindfulness to understand what makes you uncomfortable or stressed. Techniques for identifying boundary needs include journaling about situations where you felt overwhelmed or taken advantage of and noting your physical and emotional reactions. Once you clearly understand your boundaries, the next step is mindful communication. This means expressing your boundaries in a calm and respectful manner. For example, if you need some alone time after work to unwind, you might say, "I need some quiet time for myself after work to relax. I'll join you for dinner afterward." This approach ensures your needs are met without causing unnecessary conflict.

Examples of healthy boundaries in action can be incredibly inspiring. Take, for instance, a friend who struggled with work-life balance. She realized she needed to set clear boundaries with her boss about after-hours communication. After some reflection, she decided to talk with her boss, explaining that she would not be available for work-related calls or emails after 7 PM. This boundary allowed her to spend quality time with her family and reduced her stress levels significantly. Another example is a colleague who set boundaries with a friend who often vented about personal problems, leaving her emotionally drained. She compassionately communicated her need for space and proposed setting specific times for their chats, ensuring she could provide support without feeling overwhelmed.

Saying no mindfully and compassionately is an art that requires practice. Many of us struggle with saying no because we fear disappointing others or facing conflict. However, it's possible to refuse requests with kindness and without guilt. Scripts for compassionate refusal can be helpful. For example, suppose a colleague asks you to take on an extra project, and you're already overwhelmed. In that case, you might say, "I appreciate you thinking of me for this project, but I'm currently at capacity with my workload. I won't be able to give it the attention it deserves." This response is respectful and considerate while firmly setting your boundaries. Techniques for handling pushback include staying calm, reiterating your boundaries, and offering alternatives if possible. For instance, "I understand this project is important, but I can't take it on now. Perhaps we can revisit it next month, or I can help you find someone else to assist."

Personal stories of assertive boundary setting can provide valuable insights and encouragement. A close friend of mine used to feel obligated to attend every family gathering, even when it exhausted her. She set boundaries around these events after practicing mindfulness and reflecting on her needs. She told her family that she would attend major celebrations but needed downtime on other weekends. Although initially challenging, her family eventually respected her boundaries, and she felt more balanced and less stressed.

Maintaining boundaries consistently over time is crucial for their effectiveness. Regular boundary check-ins help ensure your boundaries are still serving you well. Set aside time to reflect on your boundaries and whether they need adjustment. Mindfulness practices for reinforcing boundaries include meditation and self-reflection exercises that help you stay connected to your needs. Techniques for adjusting boundaries as needed involve being flexible and open to change. Life circumstances can evolve, and your boundaries may need to shift accordingly. For example, you may need to tighten your boundaries during particularly stressful periods or relax when you have more capacity.

Incorporating these mindful practices into your life can help you establish and maintain healthy boundaries, reduce stress, and enhance your overall well-being. By being clear about your needs and communicating them compassionately, you can create a balanced and fulfilling life.

Mindful Parenting Techniques

I remember the moment vividly. My toddler was having a full-blown meltdown in the middle of the grocery store, and I felt all eyes on me. My stress levels were through the roof. At that moment, I took a deep breath and tried something new: mindfulness. I focused on my breath, grounded myself, and responded to my child calmly and empathetically. At that moment, I changed my approach to parenting forever.

Mindfulness can profoundly enhance your parenting skills and improve parent-child relationships. The benefits of mindful parenting are numerous. Being fully present with your children can foster deeper connections, improve communication, and create a more peaceful home environment. Mindfulness helps you respond to your child's needs with patience and understanding rather than reacting out of frustration or stress. Real-life examples abound. Consider a mother who practices mindfulness during her morning routine with her kids. Instead of rushing through breakfast, she takes time to engage with them, listen to their stories, and share their excitement for the day. This simple practice sets a positive tone for the family and strengthens their bond.

One of the key elements of mindful parenting is mindful communication with your children. Active listening exercises can help you truly hear and understand your child's thoughts and feelings. When your child speaks, focus entirely on them. Make eye contact, nod in acknowledgment, and refrain from interrupting. This practice shows your child that their voice matters and builds trust. Techniques for empathetic responses are equally important. Reflect on what your child has said to show understanding. For instance, if your child says, "I'm scared of the dark," you might respond, "It sounds like the dark makes you feel uncomfortable. What can we do to help you feel better?" Scripts for mindful conversations can guide you through challenging discussions. When addressing a conflict, use "I" statements to express your feelings and needs without blaming them. For example, "I feel worried when you don't finish your homework because I want you to succeed. How can we work together to make sure it gets done?"

Parenting is inherently stressful, but mindfulness practices can help manage these challenges. Mindful breathing exercises for parents offer a quick way to calm your mind and body. Take a few deep breaths, focusing on the sensation of air entering and leaving your lungs. This simple practice can reduce stress and help you respond to your child's needs with greater patience. Techniques for staying calm during tantrums are invaluable. When your child is in a meltdown, try grounding yourself by feeling the floor beneath your feet and taking slow, deep breaths. This can help you maintain your composure and handle the situation more effectively. Self-compassion practices for parenting guilt are also crucial. It's easy to feel guilty when you don't meet your high standards as a parent. Remind yourself that it's okay to be imperfect. Offer yourself the same kindness and understanding you would extend to a friend in a similar situation.

Creating mindful family practices can further enhance your parenting and family dynamics. Family mindfulness meditation sessions can be a wonderful way to bond and cultivate a sense of calm together. Choose a quiet time before bed, and guide your family through a short meditation. Focus on the breath, body sensations, or a calming visualization. This practice can help everyone unwind and connect on a deeper level. Mindful eating as a family is another great practice. During meals, encourage everyone to pay attention to the food's flavors, textures, and smells. Share what you appreciate about the meal and express gratitude for the nourishment. This can transform mealtime into a mindful and enjoyable family ritual. A family mindfulness corner can provide a dedicated space for these practices. Choose a cozy spot in your home, add some cushions, calming decorations, and perhaps a few mindfulness tools like a singing bowl or essential oils. This space can serve as a sanctuary for family members to retreat to when they need a moment of calm.

Mindful parenting is not about being a perfect parent. It's about being present, compassionate, and responsive to your child's needs. Incorporating these mindful techniques into your daily routine can create a more harmonious and connected family life.

Finding Peace Amidst Chaos

Life can often feel like a whirlwind, with responsibilities tugging at you from every direction. Finding moments of peace and mindfulness during this chaos can seem nearly impossible, but it's achievable with the right techniques. Quick mindfulness breaks can be your lifeline. These are short pauses where you take a moment to center yourself. Close your eyes, take a few deep breaths, and focus on the sensation of the air filling your lungs. Even just 30 seconds of mindful breathing can make a significant difference. Another technique is to engage in a sensory check-in. Notice what you see, hear, smell, taste, and feel. This simple practice can ground you in the present moment and calm you.

Finding peace in everyday activities is another powerful way to integrate mindfulness into your life. Washing dishes, for example, can become a meditative practice. Pay attention to the water's warmth, the soap's feel, and the running tap's sound. This turns a mundane chore into a moment of mindfulness. A personal story that comes to mind is when I started practicing mindful walking on my way to work. Instead of rushing, I focused on the sensation of my feet hitting the pavement and the rhythm of my steps. This simple shift transformed my commute from a stressful rush to a peaceful start to my day.

Creating mindful spaces at home can also promote a sense of calm and tranquility. Setting up a home mindfulness corner doesn't require much space—just a small area where you can retreat for a few minutes of peace. Add a comfortable cushion, calming decorations, and perhaps a plant. The presence of natural elements like plants or water features can enhance the calming effect. Declutter techniques mindfully involve sorting items into categories: keep, donate, and discard. A clutter-free space can significantly reduce stress and create an environment conducive to mindfulness.

Practicing mindfulness on the go is essential for those of us with busy schedules. Mindful driving techniques can transform your commute into a peaceful experience. Focus on the sensation of your hands on the steering wheel, the rhythm of your breath, and the sights around you. Instead of getting frustrated with traffic, use that time to practice mindfulness. Walking meditation in busy environments is another way to stay centered. As you walk through a crowded street, focus on each step, the movement of your body, and the sounds around you. Using mindfulness apps on the go can provide guided practices and reminders to stay present, making it easier to incorporate mindfulness into your daily routine.

Cultivating a mindful attitude means integrating mindfulness into every aspect of your life, not just during formal practices. Practicing gratitude daily can shift your focus from what's wrong to what's right. Take a moment to reflect on three things you're grateful for each day. This simple practice can bring a sense of positivity and contentment. Techniques for mindful reflection at the end of the day involve reviewing your day with a non-judgmental attitude. Consider what went well, what challenges you faced, and how you handled them. Inspirational quotes and affirmations for daily mindfulness can serve as gentle reminders to stay present. Write down a few of your favorite quotes and place them where you'll see them often, such as on your bathroom mirror or computer screen.

Incorporating these practices into your life can help you find moments of peace and mindfulness, even amidst the chaos. By creating mindful spaces, practicing mindfulness on the go, and cultivating a mindful attitude, you can navigate the demands of daily life with greater ease and calm. This chapter has provided practical tools and techniques to balance your roles and responsibilities mindfully, reducing stress and enhancing your overall well-being.

EIGHT

Living in the Present Moment

I remember a summer afternoon when I sat in my backyard, watching my children play. My mind would have been racing about work deadlines, household chores, and future plans. But that day, something shifted. I decided to immerse myself fully in the moment. I noticed the vibrant colors of the flowers, the sound of laughter, and the sun's warmth on my skin. I felt a profound sense of peace and contentment for the first time in a long while. This experience taught me the transformative power of living in the present.

The Power of Now: Staying Present

Understanding Present-Moment Awareness: Living in the present moment, often referred to as present-moment awareness, means fully engaging with the here and now. It involves paying attention to your current experience rather than dwelling on the past or worrying about the future. This simple yet profound practice can significantly enhance your psychological and emotional well-being. Research shows that being present can lower stress levels, improve mood, and increase overall life satisfaction.

When you're present, you're not bogged down by regrets about the past or anxieties about the future. Instead, you experience life with all its beauty and imperfections as it unfolds. This can lead to greater emotional resilience, as you're better equipped to handle whatever comes your way without the added burden of past and future worries. Being present allows you to fully appreciate the small joys of life, which often go unnoticed when your mind is elsewhere.

Techniques for Staying Present: One of the most effective ways to stay anchored in the present is through mindful breathing exercises. These exercises help you connect with your breath, always in the here and now. Try this: Sit comfortably, close your eyes, and take a deep breath through your nose. Feel the air fill your lungs, and then slowly exhale through your mouth. Focus solely on the sensation of breathing, and let any wandering thoughts drift away.

Another powerful technique is using sensory awareness to stay grounded. Pay attention to the details around you—the texture of the fabric you're sitting on, the sounds in your environment, the taste of your food. Engaging your senses helps bring your mind back to the present moment. You can also redirect wandering thoughts by gently acknowledging them and then shifting your focus to what you are doing.

The Role of Acceptance: Acceptance plays a crucial role in staying present. It means embracing the present moment without trying to change or judge it. This non-judgmental awareness allows you to experience life more fully and respond to situations more clearly and calmly. Acceptance doesn't mean resignation; it means acknowledging reality without resistance.

Practicing acceptance can be challenging, especially when faced with difficult emotions or situations. But by accepting what is, you free yourself from the struggle against reality. Techniques for practicing acceptance include mindfulness meditation, where you observe your thoughts and feelings without getting caught up in them. You might say, "It's okay to feel this way. This moment is as it is." This simple acknowledgment can create a sense of peace and reduce the urge to control everything.

Real-Life Applications: Staying present can enhance various aspects of your life. At work, being present can improve focus and productivity. When fully engaged in a task, you're more likely to perform it efficiently and effectively. This focused attention can lead to better work quality and greater job satisfaction.

Being present fosters deeper connections in personal relationships. When you listen to someone with full attention without thinking about what to say next or getting distracted, you create a space for genuine understanding and empathy. This mindful communication can strengthen your relationships and make interactions more meaningful.

Finally, staying present helps you find joy in everyday activities. Whether it's savoring a meal, enjoying a walk, or playing with your children, being fully engaged in these moments can bring a sense of fulfillment and happiness. You begin to appreciate the richness of life's simple pleasures, often overlooked in daily life's rush.

Reflection Exercise: Savoring the Moment

Take a moment to reflect on a recent experience where you felt fully present. What were you doing? How did it feel? Write down your thoughts and consider how to bring more of these moments into your daily life.

Living in the present moment is a powerful practice that can transform your life. By embracing the here and now, you can reduce stress, improve your well-being, and find deeper connection and joy in your everyday experiences.

Letting Go of the Past

The past has a way of clinging to us, like an old coat we can't seem to shed. You might find yourself replaying past mistakes or regretting missed opportunities. This emotional weight can be heavy, making it hard to move forward. Past regrets and grudges can hinder your present happiness, keeping you in a negative cycle. Holding onto these feelings can also contribute to current stress, as unresolved issues from the past often manifest as anxiety or emotional turmoil in the present. Recognizing how these past experiences affect your well-being is the first step toward freeing yourself from their grip.

Mindfulness techniques can be incredibly effective in helping you release the hold of the past. Guided meditations for letting go can provide a structured way to process and release these lingering emotions. Close your eyes, take a deep breath, and visualize a moment you're struggling to let go of from your past. Picture it as a cloud drifting away, getting smaller and smaller until it disappears. This visualization can help you emotionally distance yourself from past events. Journaling exercises are another powerful tool. Write about your past experiences, allowing yourself to express your feelings fully. This act of writing can be cathartic, helping you process and make sense of your emotions. Visualizations for release and healing, such as imagining a healing light washing over you, can also facilitate emotional release and bring peace.

Forgiveness and self-compassion play crucial roles in letting go of the past. Practicing self-forgiveness allows you to acknowledge your mistakes without harsh self-judgment. One effective technique is to write a letter to yourself, offering the same kindness and understanding you would extend to a friend. This can help you move past self-blame and cultivate a sense of self-acceptance. Cultivating compassion for others is equally important. Holding onto grudges can be a heavy burden, but practicing compassion can lighten this load. Try to see the situation from the other person's perspective and understand their actions within the context of their struggles. Real-life stories of healing through forgiveness can be inspiring. Consider the story of a woman who forgave her estranged father after years of resentment. This act of forgiveness healed their relationship and brought her a profound sense of inner peace.

Moving forward involves setting intentions for the future and creating rituals for closure. Setting intentions can provide a sense of direction and purpose. Write down your intentions, focusing on the positive changes you want to make. Creating rituals for closure, such as lighting a candle or saying a prayer, can symbolize letting go of the past and embracing the present. Practicing gratitude for the present moment is another powerful strategy. Each day, take a moment to reflect on what you're grateful for. This can shift your focus from past regrets to present blessings, fostering a sense of contentment and peace.

Exercise: Writing a Letter of Forgiveness

Find a quiet space and take a few deep breaths to center yourself. Write a letter to someone from your past whom you need to forgive. You don't have to send it. Just the act of writing can help you process your feelings and find closure.

By recognizing the impact of the past, practicing mindfulness techniques, and embracing forgiveness and self-compassion, you can release the hold of past experiences and move forward with a lighter heart and a clearer mind.

Reducing Worry About the Future

Worrying about the future is something we all do, but it can be particularly intense for those of us who struggle with anxiety. Future anxiety stems from our brain's natural tendency to predict and plan. While this can be helpful, it often spirals into a cycle of worry when we fixate on potential problems or uncertainties. This kind of anxiety can be triggered by various factors—upcoming deadlines, financial concerns, health issues, or even the state of the world. When left unchecked, worrying about the future can significantly impact our mental health, leading to increased stress, insomnia, and even physical symptoms like headaches or digestive issues.

One of the most effective ways to manage future anxiety is through mindfulness practices. Simple guided breathing exercises can provide immediate relief. Find a quiet space, sit comfortably, and take a deep breath through your nose. Hold it for a moment, then slowly exhale through your mouth. Repeat this process several times, focusing solely on your breath. This can help calm your mind and body, reducing the intensity of your worries. Visualization techniques can also be incredibly soothing. Close your eyes and picture a peaceful scene—perhaps a serene beach or a quiet forest. Imagine yourself there, feeling safe and relaxed. This mental escape can help alleviate fears about the future.

Mindful journaling is another powerful tool for addressing future concerns. Set aside a few minutes each day to write about your worries. Be honest and specific about what's troubling you. Then, list possible solutions or steps you can take to address these concerns. This practice helps you process your emotions and brings clarity and perspective. You might find that some worries are not as daunting as they initially seemed, and others may have actionable steps you can take to mitigate them.

Cultivating trust in the process of life and practicing patience are essential for reducing future anxiety. It's about building trust in yourself and the universe. One technique for building this trust is to reflect on past challenges you've overcome. Remind yourself that you have navigated difficulties before and have the strength to do so again. Exercises for practicing patience can be woven into your daily life. For instance, when you find yourself in a situation that tests your patience—like waiting in line or dealing with a slow internet connection—take a deep breath and remind yourself that it's okay to wait. These small moments of patience can build your resilience over time.

Personal stories can be incredibly inspiring. I recall a friend who was facing a significant career transition. She was worried about whether she would find a new job that matched her skills and passions. By practicing mindfulness and cultivating trust, she learned to focus on the steps she could control, like updating her resume and networking. Over time, she found a job that she loved and realized that her worries, while valid, did not define her path. This experience underscored the importance of trusting the process and being patient with ourselves.

Shifting your focus from future worries to present-moment awareness can be a game-changer. One effective strategy is to redirect anxious thoughts when they arise. When you catch yourself worrying about the future, gently bring your attention back to the present moment. You might say to yourself, "Right now, I am safe. Right now, I am okay." Mindful activities can also help anchor you in the present. Engage in activities that require your full attention, like cooking, gardening, or drawing. These activities can provide a mental break from future worries and help you stay grounded.

Creating a daily mindfulness practice can further support your efforts to stay present. Start your day with a short meditation, focusing on your breath, or a calming mantra. Throughout the day, take mindful breaks to check in with yourself and reset your focus. Even a few minutes of mindfulness can make a significant difference. Integrating these practices into your routine allows you to gradually shift your mindset from future-focused anxiety to present-moment awareness, finding peace and balance in your daily life.

Practicing Mindfulness in Everyday Activities

Incorporating mindfulness into your daily routine doesn't require grand gestures. It's about finding moments of presence in the mundane. When I first started practicing mindfulness, I discovered that everyday tasks could become opportunities for mindfulness. Cooking, for instance, became a meditative experience. As I chopped vegetables, I focused on the rhythm of the knife, the vibrant colors, and the fresh scents. Each step in the process grounded me in the present moment, transforming a routine chore into a source of calm and satisfaction.

Household chores can also become mindful activities. Whether you're washing dishes, folding laundry, or sweeping the floor, paying full attention to the task at hand can be surprisingly soothing. Feel the warm water on your hands, the fabric's texture, or the broom's movement. By immersing yourself in these sensations, you can quiet your mind and find a sense of peace in the simplicity of the task. Mindful commuting is another way to bring mindfulness into your daily life. Instead of stressing about traffic or getting lost in thought, focus on the sensations of driving or walking. Notice the sights, sounds, and smells around you. This shift in focus can turn your commute from a stressful experience into a mindful journey.

Mindful communication is essential for building deeper, more meaningful connections. Active listening exercises can transform how you interact with others. When someone is speaking to you, give them your full attention. Make eye contact, nod, and avoid interrupting. This shows respect and allows you to understand their perspective fully. Techniques for mindful speaking involve pausing before you respond, choosing your words carefully, and speaking with intention. Reflective listening practices can further enhance your interactions. Reflect on what you heard after someone shares their thoughts to ensure understanding. Phrases like "What I hear you saying is..." can clarify communication and deepen your connection.

Leisure activities offer another opportunity for mindfulness. Mindful reading, for example, involves immersing yourself fully in the text. Pay attention to the words, the emotions they evoke, and the imagery they create. This focused attention can make reading a more enriching experience. Similarly, practicing mindfulness during exercise can enhance your physical and mental well-being. Whether you're running, doing yoga, or lifting weights, focus on your breath, the movement of your body, and the sensations you feel. This not only improves your performance but also makes exercise more enjoyable. Mindful creative activities like painting or crafting can also be deeply fulfilling. Lose yourself in the process, noticing your creativity's colors, textures, and flow.

Creating mindful rituals can anchor your day in moments of presence and calm. A morning mindfulness routine can set a positive tone for the day. Start with a few minutes of meditation or deep breathing, then set an intention for the day. This practice can help you approach your day with clarity and purpose. Evening wind-down practices are equally important. Spend a few minutes reflecting on your day, acknowledging your accomplishments, and letting go of any lingering stress. Consider incorporating gentle stretches or soothing tea into your evening routine. Mindful moments throughout the day can sustain your practice. Take a few deep breaths before starting a new task, pause to appreciate a beautiful view, or savor the taste of your food. These small moments of mindfulness can accumulate, creating a more peaceful and centered life.

Exercise: Creating a Mindful Morning Routine

Start your day with intention. Spend five minutes each morning in silence, focusing on your breath. Set an intention for how you want to approach your day. Notice how this practice influences your mood and productivity.

Incorporating mindfulness into everyday activities can transform your routine, making each moment an opportunity for presence and peace. Practicing mindfulness in routine tasks, communication, leisure activities, and daily rituals can create a life filled with deeper connections, greater satisfaction, and lasting tranquility.

NINE

Guided Meditations for Specific Needs

I remember one particularly hectic day. Work was overwhelming, my kids demanded my attention, and my to-do list seemed endless. By late afternoon, I felt like I was about to implode. My shoulders were tense, my head was pounding, and I couldn't focus on anything. That's when I decided to try a guided meditation for stress relief. I found a quiet corner, closed my eyes, and followed the soothing voice guiding me through deep breathing and visualization. In just a few minutes, I felt a wave of calm wash over me, and the tension began to melt away. This experience showed me firsthand how powerful stress relief meditation can be.

Introduction to Stress Relief Meditation

Stress is a common part of life but often affects the body and mind. When stressed, your body goes into fight-or-flight mode, releasing stress hormones like cortisol. This response was useful for our ancestors when facing immediate dangers, but in modern life, it can lead to chronic stress and a host of related issues. Stress can manifest physically through headaches, muscle tension, and digestive problems. Emotionally, it can result in anxiety, irritability, and even depression.

Meditation offers a powerful antidote to stress. Meditation can counteract the stress response by focusing your mind and calming your body. It lowers cortisol levels, slows your heart rate, and helps relax your muscles. This practice can create a state of deep relaxation and mental clarity, allowing you to tackle life's challenges with a more balanced mindset.

Preparation for Meditation

Preparing your body and mind before you begin the meditation is important. First, find a quiet, comfortable space where you won't be disturbed. This could be a cozy corner of your home, a quiet room, or even a peaceful spot in your garden. The key is to choose a place where you feel safe and relaxed.

Setting a calming ambiance can enhance the meditation experience. Soft lighting, such as a dim lamp or candles, can create a soothing environment. Consider playing gentle, instrumental music or nature sounds to block background noise. Using props like cushions or blankets can also add to your comfort. Sit or lie comfortably, perhaps with a cushion supporting your back or a blanket draped over your legs.

Step-by-Step Meditation Guide

Now that you're ready, let's dive into the stress relief meditation. Start by closing your eyes and taking a few deep breaths. Inhale deeply through your nose, allowing your abdomen to expand, and then exhale slowly through your mouth. Repeat this a few times to center yourself and begin relaxing your body.

Next, we'll practice progressive muscle relaxation. Starting with your toes, tense the muscles for a few seconds and then release. Move up to your calves, thighs, and so on until you've tensed and relaxed each muscle group in your body. This technique helps release built-up tension and prepares your body for deeper relaxation.

Now, let's move into visualization. Imagine yourself in a peaceful place that brings you joy and tranquility. It could be a beach with gentle waves lapping at the shore, a lush forest with birds chirping, or a serene mountain top with a cool breeze. Picture every detail vividly —the colors, sounds, smells, and sensations. As you immerse yourself in this visualization, let any remaining tension melt away. Stay in this peaceful place for a few minutes, enjoying the sense of calm and relaxation.

Post-Meditation Practices

After the meditation, it's important to mindfully transition back to your day. Start with some gentle stretching exercises to awaken your body. Stretch your arms overhead, roll your shoulders, and gently twist your torso from side to side. These movements can help release any residual tension and re-energize you.

Consider drinking a cup of herbal tea to enhance your sense of calm further. Chamomile, lavender, or peppermint tea can be particularly soothing. As you sip your tea, take a moment to savor the warmth and flavor, practicing mindfulness by fully engaging with the experience.

Finally, take a few minutes to journal about your meditation experience. Reflect on how you felt before, during, and after the meditation. Note any physical or emotional changes you observed. Journaling can reinforce the benefits of meditation and provide a valuable record of your progress.

Guided meditation for stress relief can be a powerful tool for navigating life's challenges with greater ease and resilience. By incorporating these practices into your routine, you can create calm and clear moments, deepening your inner peace.

Guided Meditation for Self-Compassion

Self-compassion meditation is a powerful tool for fostering self-love and acceptance. It's not just about being kind to yourself superficially; it's about fundamentally changing how you relate to yourself, especially in moments of struggle. Self-compassion plays a crucial role in mental health by helping you respond to your suffering with kindness rather than harsh judgment. This practice can be transformative. It teaches you to treat yourself with the same care and understanding you would offer a close friend.

Imagine waking up each morning, and instead of criticizing yourself for not doing enough, you gently remind yourself that you're doing your best. Picture facing a difficult situation, and instead of berating yourself for feeling anxious, you place a hand over your heart and offer yourself words of encouragement. Self-compassion meditation fosters these moments of self-love, helping you to embrace your imperfections and see them as part of the shared human experience.

I've seen firsthand how self-compassion meditation can change lives. A friend who constantly struggled with feelings of inadequacy began practicing it. Over time, she started to notice a shift. She became more patient with herself, more forgiving of her mistakes, and more resilient in the face of challenges. Another woman I know, dealing with the aftermath of a painful divorce, found solace in self-compassion meditation. It helped her heal from the emotional wounds and rebuild her self-worth.

Creating a safe and nurturing environment is key to getting the most out of your self-compassion meditation practice. Start by choosing a quiet and private location where you won't be disturbed. This could be a cozy corner of your bedroom, a peaceful spot in your living room, or even a secluded area in your garden. Surround yourself with soft, comforting items like blankets, cushions, or a favorite stuffed animal. These items can provide a sense of security and comfort, helping you to relax more deeply.

Setting an intention for your meditation session can also be incredibly helpful. Before you begin, take a moment to reflect on what you hope to achieve. You may want to cultivate more self-love, find forgiveness for past mistakes, or offer yourself some kindness in a difficult moment. Setting an intention can give your meditation a sense of purpose and direction.

To begin the self-compassion meditation, start with mindful breathing to center your mind. Sit comfortably, close your eyes, and take a few deep breaths. Inhale deeply through your nose, feeling your abdomen expand, and then exhale slowly through your mouth. As you breathe, allow your mind to settle and your body to relax.

Next, start silently reciting self-compassion phrases. These could be phrases like, "May I be kind to myself," "May I accept myself as I am," or "May I find peace in my heart." Repeat these phrases slowly and gently, allowing their meaning to sink in. You might find it helpful to vary the phrases based on your needs.

As you breathe and recite phrases, visualize yourself surrounded by a warm, comforting light. This light represents the love and compassion you're offering to yourself. Imagine it enveloping you, filling you with warmth and peace. If it feels right, place your hands on your heart as a physical gesture of self-compassion. Feel the warmth of your hands and let it remind you that you deserve love and kindness.

Integrating self-compassion into your daily life can make a significant difference. During challenging moments, try using your self-compassion phrases. When you catch yourself in negative self-talk, pause and replace those critical thoughts with words of kindness. Practicing self-compassion in front of a mirror can also be powerful. Look into your own eyes and speak words of encouragement and love. This might initially feel awkward, but it can help reinforce a compassionate inner dialogue.

Keeping a self-compassion journal is another great way to integrate this practice into your life. Each day, write down moments when you offered yourself kindness or times when you struggled and how you responded. Reflect on these entries and notice any patterns or changes over time. This journal can serve as a reminder of your progress and a tool for deepening your self-compassion practice.

Guided Meditation for Emotional Balance

Emotional balance is crucial for overall well-being. It helps you navigate life's ups and downs with grace and resilience. You might feel overwhelmed, irritable, or anxious when your emotions are out of balance. These imbalances can affect your relationships, work, and physical health. Emotional balance meditation helps you maintain a steady emotional state, which in turn enhances your overall quality of life. Regularly practicing this type of meditation can achieve a more balanced emotional state, allowing you to respond to life's challenges calmly and clearly.

To prepare for an emotional balance meditation, creating a serene and clutter-free space is important. Choose a spot where you feel comfortable and safe. This could be a quiet corner of your home, a peaceful area in your garden, or even a dedicated meditation room. Clear away any clutter that might distract you. A tidy space can help create a sense of calm and order. Setting an intention for your meditation can also be helpful. Reflect on what you hope to achieve from the session. You may want to cultivate more patience, find inner peace, or become more aware of your emotions. Setting an intention can give your meditation a sense of purpose and direction. Using calming scents like lavender or chamomile can further enhance your meditation experience. These scents have calming properties that can help you relax and focus.

Let's move into the step-by-step guide for emotional balance meditation. Begin with grounding exercises. Sit comfortably and place your feet flat on the ground. Feel the connection between your feet and the earth. This grounding technique helps anchor you in the present moment. Next, take a few deep breaths. Inhale deeply through your nose, allowing your abdomen to expand, and then exhale slowly through your mouth. Repeat this a few times to center yourself. Now, mindfully observe your current emotions. Without judgment, acknowledge any feelings that arise. Whether it's sadness, joy, frustration, or contentment, let each emotion come and go without trying to change it. Use your breath to create a sense of balance and harmony. As you inhale, imagine drawing in calm and peace. As you exhale, visualize releasing any tension or negativity. Continue this rhythmic breathing, allowing your breath to steady your emotions.

Visualizing yourself in a state of emotional stability and calm can be incredibly powerful. Imagine yourself standing in a peaceful place, feeling balanced and centered. Picture a serene environment, whether it's a tranquil beach, a quiet forest, or a mountaintop. Envision yourself standing tall, with a sense of inner strength and calm. As you visualize this scene, let the feelings of stability and peace wash over you. Stay in this visualization for a few minutes, soaking in emotional balance and tranquility.

After completing the meditation, take some time for post-meditation reflection. Journaling about your current emotional state can deepen your understanding and awareness. Write down any emotions you observed during the meditation and how you felt before and after the session. Reflect on the impact of the meditation. Did you notice any shifts in your emotional state? Were there any particular emotions that stood out? Setting intentions for maintaining emotional balance can also be helpful. Think about how you can carry balance and calm into your daily life. Write down any intentions or affirmations that resonate with you. This practice can reinforce the benefits of meditation and support your ongoing emotional well-being.

By regularly practicing emotional balance meditation, you can develop a greater sense of emotional stability and resilience. This practice can help you navigate life's challenges with a calm and balanced mind, enhancing your overall well-being and inner peace.

Guided Meditation for Sleep

When I first tried sleep meditation, I was desperate for rest. Nights were filled with tossing and turning, my mind racing with worries and unfinished tasks. Like many women juggling multiple roles, I needed help to wind down. Sleep meditation became my sanctuary, a gentle way to transition from the day's chaos to a peaceful night's rest. The primary purpose of sleep meditation is to prepare your body and mind for restful sleep. It helps quiet the mental chatter, reduce stress, and create a relaxation conducive to deep, restorative sleep.

Poor sleep impacts every aspect of health. It can lead to irritability, difficulty concentrating, and weakened immune function. Chronic sleep deprivation is linked to more serious issues like heart disease, depression, and obesity. Meditation offers a natural way to improve sleep quality by calming the mind and relaxing the body. Through focused attention and deep breathing, meditation helps to lower the heart rate, reduce muscle tension, and signal to your body that it's time to sleep.

Creating a sleep-inducing environment is crucial for effective sleep meditation. Start by ensuring your sleeping space is dark, quiet, and cool. Darkness signals to your brain that it's time to produce melatonin, the hormone that regulates sleep. Blackout curtains or an eye mask can help block out light. Silence is equally important. Use earplugs or a white noise machine to drown out disruptive sounds. Soft, soothing music can also create a calming atmosphere. Incorporating scents like lavender or chamomile can further enhance relaxation. These scents are known for their calming properties and can help create a sense of tranquility.

To begin the sleep meditation, start with a body scan to release tension. Lie down comfortably on your bed and close your eyes. Take a few deep breaths, focusing on the sensation of air entering and leaving your lungs. Begin by directing your attention to your toes. Notice any tension or discomfort and consciously relax that area. Gradually move your focus through your body—your feet, legs, hips, abdomen, chest, arms, and head. As you scan each area, breathe deeply and release any tension.

Next, practice deep, slow breathing to calm your mind. Inhale deeply through your nose, filling your lungs completely. Hold your breath for a moment, then exhale slowly through your mouth. Repeat this process several times, making each breath slower and deeper. This breathing technique helps to lower your heart rate and create a sense of calm.

Now, visualize a peaceful, sleep-inducing scene. Imagine floating on a soft, fluffy cloud, gently swaying with the breeze. Feel the cloud supporting your body, cradling you in comfort. Picture the sky above, filled with twinkling stars, and feel the cool, fresh air on your skin. As you immerse yourself in this visualization, let any remaining tension melt away. Continue to breathe deeply, syncing your breath with the gentle movement of the cloud.

Using affirmations for restful sleep can further enhance the meditation. Silently repeat phrases like, "I am calm and ready for sleep," "My mind is at peace," or "I release the worries of the day."

These affirmations help to reinforce a sense of calm and readiness for sleep.

Maintaining a consistent sleep routine is essential for good sleep hygiene. Try to go to bed and wake up simultaneously every day, even on weekends. This helps regulate your body's internal clock. Avoid screens and stimulating activities before bed. The blue light from screens can interfere with melatonin production, making it harder to fall asleep. Instead, use calming activities like reading a book, taking a warm bath, or practicing gentle yoga or stretching. These activities can help signal your body that it's time to wind down.

Incorporating sleep meditation into your nightly routine can transform your sleep experience. By creating a sleep-inducing environment, practicing guided meditation techniques, and maintaining a consistent sleep schedule, you can improve the quality of your sleep and wake up feeling refreshed and rejuvenated.

Let's explore how integrating mindfulness into daily routines can create lasting peace and balance as we move forward.

TEN

Mindfulness During Life Transitions

Life is full of transitions, and one of the most challenging can be losing a job. I remember a time when I faced this difficult experience. Walking out of the office for the last time, I felt fear, anger, and sadness. The uncertainty of what lay ahead was overwhelming. I realized that to move forward, I needed to acknowledge and process these emotions mindfully. This chapter aims to guide you through this unsettling time with mindfulness techniques to help you manage the emotional upheaval and maintain your self-worth.

Coping with Job Loss

Losing a job can stir up a whirlwind of emotions. It's essential to mindfully acknowledge and process these feelings rather than suppress them. Start by identifying and labeling your emotions. Are you feeling angry, scared, or perhaps ashamed? Naming these feelings can help you understand and manage them better. This practice is known as emotional granularity, which involves being precise about your feelings. Instead of saying, "I'm upset," try to articulate, "I'm feeling frustrated and anxious about my financial stability." This clarity can reduce the intensity of your emotions by making them more manageable.

In moments of heightened emotional intensity, mindful breathing exercises can be incredibly grounding. Close your eyes and take a deep breath through your nose, feeling your lungs expand. Hold it for a moment, then exhale slowly through your mouth. Repeat this process a few times, focusing solely on the sensation of your breath. This simple act can help bring you back to the present moment, reducing the intensity of your emotions and offering a sense of calm amidst the chaos.

Journaling is another powerful tool for reflecting on your job loss experience. Set aside a few minutes daily to write about your thoughts and feelings. Don't worry about grammar or structure; just let your emotions flow onto the paper. You might write about the initial shock, the fears about the future, or even the small moments of hope you encounter. This practice can provide a safe space to process your emotions and gain insights into your experience. Over time, you may notice patterns or themes that can guide your healing process.

Maintaining your self-worth during job loss is crucial. It's easy to fall into the trap of equating your job with your value but remember, you are so much more than your employment status. Practice self-compassion by offering yourself the kindness and understanding you would give a friend in a similar situation. When feelings of failure arise, counteract them with self-compassion exercises. For instance, place your hand on your heart and gently remind yourself, "It's okay to feel this way. I am doing my best, and this situation does not define my worth."

Affirmations can also significantly reinforce self-worth. Create a set of affirmations that resonate with you, such as "I am capable and resilient" or "I have valuable skills and talents." Repeat these affirmations daily, especially during moments of doubt. This practice can help rewire your brain to focus on your strengths and potential rather than your perceived shortcomings.

Visualization techniques can further support your self-worth by helping you envision future success. Find a quiet place to sit comfortably, close your eyes, and take a few deep breaths. Imagine yourself thriving in a new job or career that excites and fulfills you. Picture the details—what you're doing, your environment, and the people you're working with. Allow yourself to feel the emotions associated with this success—joy, pride, and satisfaction. Visualization can create a mental blueprint for your goals, making them feel more attainable.

Staying present and focused can be particularly challenging during job loss, as worries about the future often dominate your thoughts. Incorporate mindful job search practices to keep you grounded. Set specific times for job hunting and related activities; use that time mindfully. Focus on one task at a time, whether updating your resume, writing a cover letter, or searching for job openings. This focused approach can prevent you from feeling overwhelmed and increase your productivity.

Managing anxiety about future employment is another critical aspect. Techniques such as mindful breathing and grounding exercises can help. For example, before an interview, take a few moments to practice deep breathing or the 5-4-3-2-1 grounding technique: identify five things you can see, four you can touch, three you can hear, two you can smell, and one you can taste. These practices can help calm your nerves and keep you focused on the present moment.

Establishing a new daily routine incorporating mindfulness can provide structure and stability during this uncertain time. Start by setting a regular schedule for job search activities. Dedicate specific hours of the day to searching for jobs, networking, or enhancing your skills. Include mindfulness breaks throughout the day to prevent burnout and maintain emotional well-being. During these breaks, practice a quick meditation, take a mindful walk, or take a few deep breaths.

Mindful morning and evening routines can further support your well-being. In the morning, start your day with a few minutes of meditation or deep breathing to set a positive tone. Reflect on your intentions for the day and visualize positive outcomes. In the evening, wind down with a gratitude practice. Reflect on three things you are grateful for, no matter how small. This practice can shift your focus from what you lack to what you have, fostering a sense of contentment and peace.

Losing a job is undeniably challenging, but with these mindfulness practices, you can navigate this transition with greater ease and resilience. By acknowledging and processing your emotions, maintaining your self-worth, staying present and focused, and creating a new routine, you can find a sense of stability and inner peace amidst the uncertainty.

Navigating Relationship Changes

Navigating relationship changes can be one of life's most challenging experiences. Whether it's the end of a romantic relationship, shifts in friendships, or evolving family dynamics, these changes can stir up a whirlwind of emotions. Mindful communication is one of the most effective ways to manage these transitions. When emotions run high, it's easy to miscommunicate or avoid communication altogether. Practicing active listening can make a world of difference. This means fully focusing on the other person when they speak, resisting the urge to interrupt, and reflecting on what you've heard. For instance, instead of immediately responding with your own perspective, you might say, "I hear that you're feeling hurt because I didn't call you back. I understand how that could be frustrating."

Expressing your own emotions mindfully is equally important. Techniques such as using "I" statements can reduce conflict and foster understanding. For example, instead of saying, "You never listen to me," try, "I feel unheard when I'm interrupted." This approach focuses on your feelings rather than placing blame, making it easier for the other person to hear and understand your perspective. It helps create a space for open and honest communication, crucial for resolving conflicts and building stronger relationships.

Managing emotional overload during relationship changes is another critical aspect. Guided meditations can be incredibly helpful for calming intense emotions. Find a quiet space, close your eyes, and focus on your breath. Imagine a gentle wave washing over you, carrying away your stress and leaving you feeling calm and centered. This practice can help you regain control over your emotions, making it easier to navigate difficult conversations.

Grounding techniques can also be beneficial during emotionally charged conversations. When you feel overwhelmed, try grounding yourself by focusing on the physical sensations in your body. Place your feet firmly on the ground, feel the support of the chair beneath you, or hold a comforting object. These simple actions can help you stay present and calm, allowing you to respond thoughtfully rather than impulsively. Additionally, practicing self-compassion during these times is crucial. Offer yourself the same kindness and understanding you would give a friend in a similar situation. Remind yourself that it's okay to feel a range of emotions and that you're doing your best.

Finding inner peace amidst relationship turmoil can seem daunting, but mindfulness provides a path forward. Mindful breathing exercises are a simple yet powerful tool for finding calm. Take a few moments each day to focus on your breath. Inhale deeply through your nose, hold for a moment, and exhale slowly through your mouth. This practice can help you release tension and find a sense of tranquility, even in chaos.

Visualization techniques can also create a mental sanctuary where you can retreat when emotions become overwhelming. Close your eyes and imagine a place where you feel safe and at peace. It could be a quiet beach, a lush forest, or a cozy room. Picture every detail—the colors, sounds, scents—and allow yourself to immerse in this peaceful space. This mental escape can provide a much-needed break from the stress of relationship changes.

Daily gratitude practices can shift your focus from the turmoil to the positive aspects of your life. Each evening, reflect on three things you are grateful for, no matter how small. It could be a kind word from a friend, a beautiful sunset, or a moment of laughter. This practice helps reframe your mindset, fostering appreciation and contentment even during challenging times.

Rebuilding and moving forward after a relationship change requires intention and mindfulness. Start by setting intentions for personal growth. Reflect on what you want to achieve and how you want to grow from this experience. Write down your intentions and revisit them regularly to stay focused on your goals. Mindful journaling can be a powerful tool for processing and healing. Set aside time each day to write about your thoughts and feelings. Don't worry about structure or grammar; just let your emotions flow onto the paper. This practice can help you gain clarity and insight, making it easier to move forward.

Another important step is creating a vision for the future. Take some time to imagine what you want your life to look like. Think about your goals, dreams, and aspirations. Visualize yourself achieving these goals and living the life you desire. This practice can help you stay motivated and focused on the possibilities ahead.

Embracing Health Challenges

Health challenges can be daunting, but practicing mindful acceptance can help you navigate this difficult terrain. Accepting the present moment without judgment involves acknowledging your current state without wishing it were different. For instance, if you're dealing with chronic pain, instead of focusing on how unfair it feels, try to observe the sensations objectively. Techniques like the body scan meditation can be particularly helpful. Lie down in a comfortable position, close your eyes, and slowly bring your attention to each part of your body, starting from your toes and moving up to your head. As you focus on each area, notice the sensations without labeling them as "good" or "bad." This practice can help you develop a more neutral and accepting attitude toward your physical condition.

Guided meditations focused on acceptance can also be beneficial. Find a quiet space, sit comfortably, and close your eyes. Begin by taking a few deep breaths to center yourself. Then, imagine a soft, warm light enveloping your body, bringing a sense of peace and acceptance. As you breathe in, say to yourself, "I accept this moment as it is." As you breathe out, let go of any tension or resistance. This meditation can help you cultivate a sense of calm and acceptance, even amidst physical discomfort.

I've met individuals who have embraced their health challenges with remarkable grace. One woman I know, diagnosed with a chronic illness, used mindfulness to transform her relationship with her body. Instead of battling against her condition, she learned to work with it, focusing on what she could do rather than what she couldn't. Her story is a testament to the power of mindful acceptance in finding peace and resilience.

Managing physical pain through mindfulness requires specific techniques. As mentioned earlier, the body scan meditation can serve as a valuable tool for pain relief. By focusing on different parts of your body, you can become more aware of your pain and how it shifts and changes. This awareness can help reduce the intensity of the pain, making it more manageable.

Another effective strategy is to redirect your focus away from pain. Instead of focusing on the pain, concentrate on other sensations or activities. For example, engage in a hobby or immerse yourself in a good book. This diversion can help shift your attention away from the pain, providing temporary relief.

Mindful breathing exercises can also reduce pain perception. Sit comfortably, close your eyes, and take a deep breath in through your nose. Hold it for a moment, then exhale slowly through your mouth. As you breathe, focus on the sensation of the air entering and leaving your body. Visualize the breath as a wave of soothing energy, washing over your pain and bringing relief. Repeat this process for a few minutes, and notice how your pain levels change.

Building emotional resilience during health challenges is crucial for maintaining your mental well-being. Loving-kindness meditation can be a powerful practice for fostering resilience. Sit comfortably, close your eyes, and take a few deep breaths. Begin by silently repeating loving-kind phrases to yourself, such as "May I be healthy. May I be strong. May I be at peace." After a few minutes, extend these wishes to others, starting with loved ones and gradually including neutral people and even difficult individuals. This practice can help cultivate compassion and connection, boosting emotional resilience.

Daily affirmations can also strengthen your resilience. Create a set of affirmations that resonate with your situation, such as "I am strong and capable" or "I have the inner resources to face this challenge." Repeat these affirmations daily, especially during moments of doubt or fear. This practice can help reinforce positive beliefs about yourself and your coping ability.

Journaling prompts provide a structured way to reflect on your personal growth. Set aside time each day to write about your experiences, focusing on how you've grown and what you've learned. Prompts like "What challenges have I overcome today?" or "What strengths have I discovered in myself?" can guide your reflections and help you recognize your resilience.

Integrating mindfulness into your medical treatment and self-care routines can enhance your well-being. During medical procedures, practice mindful breathing to stay calm and centered. Focus on your breath, and let it be an anchor, grounding you in the present moment. This can help reduce anxiety and make the experience more manageable.

Staying present during doctor's appointments can also be beneficial. Before your appointment, take a few deep breaths to calm your mind. Focus on the conversation during the appointment, actively listen to your doctor, and ask questions. This mindful approach can help you stay engaged and make informed decisions about your treatment.

Creating a mindfulness-based self-care plan can further support your health journey. Include meditation, mindful breathing, and gentle yoga in your daily routine. Set aside specific times for these activities, making them a regular part of your self-care regimen. This plan can provide structure and stability, helping you navigate your health challenges with greater ease and resilience.

Finding Stability in Uncertain Times

Life can sometimes feel like an unpredictable storm, tossing you around with waves of uncertainty. Finding stability during these times can make a world of difference. Sensory grounding techniques are one of the most effective ways to ground yourself. The 5-4-3-2-1 method is a practical tool to help you refocus on the present moment. Start by identifying five things you can see around you. Next, touch four different objects and notice their textures. Listen for three distinct sounds, smell two different scents, and focus on one thing you can taste. This method engages all your senses, returning you to the here and now.

Physical grounding exercises can also provide stability. Walking barefoot on grass or sand allows you to connect with the earth and feel its stability beneath you. Another technique is to press your feet firmly into the ground while sitting or standing, feeling the support beneath you. Visualization exercises can create a mental safe haven. Close your eyes and imagine a place where you feel secure and calm. This could be a cozy room, a serene beach, or a peaceful forest. Picture every detail, from the colors to the sounds, and immerse yourself fully in this stable, safe place.

Decision-making during uncertain times can be challenging. Mindfulness can offer clarity and calmness. Before making any decision, practice mindful breathing. Take a few deep breaths, inhaling through your nose and exhaling through your mouth. This simple act can help clear your mind and reduce anxiety. Observing your thoughts without judgment is another valuable technique. When faced with a decision, take a moment to notice the thoughts that arise. Are they based on fear or rational assessment? By observing without judgment, you can gain a clearer perspective.

Guided meditations can further enhance your decision-making process. Find a quiet space, sit comfortably, and close your eyes. Focus on your breath, and as you breathe in and out, allow your mind to settle. Visualize a calm, clear lake. Imagine dropping a question or decision into the lake and watching the ripples settle. As the water becomes still again, notice any insights or clarity that arise.

This practice can help you approach decisions with a calm and focused mind.

Creating a stable daily routine is crucial for maintaining balance during uncertain times. Start by setting a regular schedule that includes mindful activities. Dedicate specific times for meditation, exercise, and relaxation. These activities provide structure and predictability, helping you easily navigate your day. Including mindfulness breaks throughout the day can prevent stress from building up. Take a few minutes to step away from your tasks, close your eyes, and focus on your breath or a calming visualization. This can help you recharge and maintain your focus.

Mindful morning and evening routines can further enhance your stability. Begin your day with a few minutes of meditation or deep breathing to set a positive tone. Reflect on your intentions for the day and visualize positive outcomes. In the evening, wind down with a gratitude practice. Reflect on three things you are grateful for, no matter how small. This practice can shift your focus from what you lack to what you have, fostering a sense of contentment and peace.

Building a support network is another essential aspect of finding stability. Mindful communication techniques can help you build and strengthen relationships. Practice active listening by fully focusing on the other person when they speak, resisting the urge to interrupt, and reflecting on what you've heard. This fosters genuine understanding and connection. Techniques for practicing empathy and active listening can further enhance your relationships. Show empathy by acknowledging the other person's feelings and offering support.

Creating a community of mindfulness practitioners can provide additional support. Join or form a mindfulness group where you can share experiences, practice together, and offer mutual support. This sense of community can provide a stable foundation during uncertain times, helping you feel connected and supported.

Finding stability in uncertain times is about grounding yourself, making clear decisions, creating a stable routine, and building a supportive network. These mindfulness practices can help you navigate life's unpredictability with greater ease and resilience. As you continue to explore these techniques, you'll find that stability and inner peace are within your reach, even amidst the chaos.

ELEVEN

Integrating Mindfulness into Daily Routines

One morning, I was rushing through my routine, unaware of what I was doing. I spilled coffee on my favorite shirt, snapped at my kids, and left the house feeling frazzled and irritable. This chaotic start set the tone for the rest of my day, leaving me anxious and overwhelmed. I realized I needed a change. That's when I decided to incorporate mindfulness into my mornings. This simple shift transformed my entire day, bringing a sense of calm and balance I desperately needed.

Morning Mindfulness Rituals

Starting your day with intention can set a positive tone, helping you navigate the challenges ahead with grace and resilience. When you wake up, rather than immediately diving into your to-do list, take a moment to set a mindful intention. This practice involves pausing to reflect on what you hope to achieve emotionally and mentally throughout the day. For instance, you may focus on staying calm during stressful moments or being fully present with your family. Setting intentions can be done through a short meditation or simply sitting quietly and thinking about your goals. Affirmations can also be powerful. Start your day with positive statements like, "I am capable," or "I approach today calmly and confidently." Reflecting on your goals during morning meditation helps solidify these intentions, creating a mental roadmap for your day.

Incorporating specific mindfulness practices into your morning routine can further enhance this sense of calm. Begin with morning breathing exercises. As soon as you wake up, sit in bed or find a comfortable spot, close your eyes, and take several deep breaths. Focus on the sensation of the air filling your lungs and the rise and fall of your chest. This simple act can ground you and set a peaceful tone for the day. Stretching or yoga with mindful awareness is another excellent practice. Spend a few minutes stretching your body, paying attention to how each movement feels. Yoga poses like the cat-cow stretch or child's pose can be particularly soothing. If you prefer a more structured routine, follow a short yoga video that emphasizes mindfulness. Even a mindful shower can become a moment of tranquility. As you wash, focus on the sensation of the water on your skin, the smell of the soap, and the sound of the water. This practice turns a mundane task into a meditative experience.

Breakfast is another opportunity to practice mindfulness and set a calm tone for the day. Instead of rushing through your meal, take time to savor each bite. Notice the flavors, textures, and smells of your food. Pay attention to the eating experience rather than letting your mind wander to your day's tasks. This can be as simple as slowly eating a piece of fruit, noticing its sweetness, and appreciating its freshness. Practicing gratitude for your meal can also enhance this experience. Before you eat, take a moment to reflect on your food journey from farm to table and express gratitude for the nourishment it provides. This small act of mindfulness can transform your breakfast into a peaceful ritual, setting a positive tone for the rest of your day.

Creating a dedicated space for morning mindfulness rituals can make these practices more effective and enjoyable. Find a quiet corner in your home where you can retreat each morning. Set up this space with cushions and candles to create a cozy and inviting atmosphere. Incorporating calming elements like plants or crystals can enhance the tranquility of your mindfulness corner. Plants bring a touch of nature indoors, providing a sense of peace and grounding. Whether you believe in their healing properties or simply appreciate their beauty, Crystals can add a soothing energy to your space. Creating a morning meditation nook doesn't require much space—just a small area to sit comfortably and focus on your breath. Having a dedicated space for mindfulness can make it easier to establish and maintain your morning rituals.

To help you incorporate these practices into your routine, here's a simple checklist for a mindful morning:

Morning Mindfulness Checklist

- Take a few deep breaths as soon as you wake up.
- Set a mindful intention for the day.
- Use positive affirmations to boost your mood.
- Spend a few minutes stretching or practicing yoga.
- Take a mindful shower, focusing on the sensations.
- Savor your breakfast, paying attention to flavors and textures.
- Express gratitude for your meal.
- Spend a few minutes in your dedicated mindfulness space.

Starting your day with these mindful practices can transform your mornings from chaotic to calm. By setting intentions, practicing mindfulness, and creating a dedicated space, you can approach each day with peace and purpose.

Mindfulness During Work Hours

The daily commute can often feel like a necessary evil, but it doesn't have to be. Whether driving, walking, or using public transportation, this time can become an opportunity for mindfulness. If you're driving, mindful driving practices can transform your experience. Focus on the feel of the steering wheel, the rhythm of your breath, and the sights around you. Pay attention to the movement of your body as you steer and accelerate, noticing how your muscles engage and relax. Listening to calming music or a mindfulness podcast can also help you stay present and relaxed during your drive.

For those who walk to work, walking meditation offers a fantastic way to start the day mindfully. As you walk, focus on each step, the movement of your body, and the sensations under your feet. Notice the rhythm of your breath and how it syncs with your steps. Pay attention to your surroundings—the chirping of birds, the rustling of leaves, the feel of the breeze. If you use public transportation, this time can also be a moment for mindfulness meditation. Find a comfortable seat, close your eyes, and focus on your breath. Notice the sounds around you without judgment, letting them come and go like waves. You can also practice body scanning to release tension from your toes and move up to your head.

Once you arrive at work, taking mindful breaks throughout the day is crucial. These breaks help you reset and maintain focus. One effective technique is mindful breathing during breaks. Close your eyes, take a deep breath through your nose, and exhale slowly through your mouth. Repeat this a few times, focusing on the sensation of your breath. This simple practice can calm your mind and reduce stress. Stretching exercises at your desk can also be beneficial. Stand up, stretch your arms overhead, roll your shoulders, and twist your torso gently. These movements release physical tension and refresh your body.

Brief meditation sessions for re-centering can be incredibly effective. Find a quiet spot, even if it's just a bathroom stall or a corner of the office. Close your eyes, take a few deep breaths, and focus on the present moment. You might visualize a peaceful scene, like a beach or a forest, to help create a mental sanctuary. These short sessions help you regain focus and approach your work calmly.

Incorporating mindfulness into your work tasks can also make a significant difference. Practicing single-tasking instead of multitasking is a great place to start. Focus on one task at a time, giving it your full attention. This approach not only increases productivity but also reduces stress. Use mindful listening during meetings. Pay attention to the speaker, make eye contact, and nod to show understanding. Avoid interrupting, and take a moment to process what you've heard before responding. This practice fosters better communication and reduces misunderstandings. Techniques for maintaining focus and reducing distractions include setting specific times for checking emails, turning off non-essential notifications, and creating a dedicated workspace free from distractions.

Managing work stress with mindfulness practices can help you maintain calm during work hours. Mindful breathing techniques, such as the 4-7-8 breathing method, can be particularly effective for stress relief. Inhale for a count of four, hold for seven and exhale for eight. This practice activates the parasympathetic nervous system, promoting relaxation. Visualization exercises for creating a mental sanctuary can also be helpful. Close your eyes and imagine a place where you feel completely at peace. It could be a beach, a forest, or a cozy room. Spend a few minutes visualizing this place, noticing the colors, sounds, and sensations. This mental escape can provide a break from stress.

Journaling about work-related stress and solutions is another powerful tool. Take a few minutes each day to write about the challenges you faced and how you responded to them. Reflect on what worked well and didn't, and consider how you might handle similar situations. This practice helps you process your experiences and fosters a proactive approach to stress management.

Integrating these mindfulness practices into your workday can transform your experience, reducing stress and enhancing your overall well-being. You can create a more balanced and fulfilling work life by approaching your commute, breaks, tasks, and stress with mindfulness.

Evening Wind-Down Practices

The transition from work to home can often feel abrupt and jarring, leaving you carrying the stress of the day into your evening. One effective way to mentally close the workday is to establish a clear boundary between work and home life. Begin by setting a specific time to stop work-related activities. At this moment, take a few minutes to sit quietly and reflect on the day. Acknowledge your accomplishments and let go of unfinished tasks, knowing they can be addressed tomorrow. This practice can help you mentally close the workday, reducing the tendency to ruminate on work issues during your time.

Practice mindful commuting as you commute home, whether by car, public transport, or walking. If you're driving, focus on the feel of the steering wheel, the rhythm of your breath, and the sights around you. Try to let go of the day's stress with each exhale. For public transport, find a seat, close your eyes if you can, and focus on your breath or the sounds around you. Walking home offers a great opportunity for walking meditation. Pay attention to each step, the movement of your body, and the sensations under your feet. These mindful commuting practices can help you transition smoothly from work to home life.

Creating a ritual to signify the end of the workday can further reinforce this transition. It could be as simple as changing your clothes, washing your face, or lighting a candle. These small acts signal to your mind and body that the workday is over and it's time to relax. For example, a friend changes into her most comfortable clothes and makes a cup of herbal tea when she gets home. This simple ritual helps her leave work behind and shift into relaxation mode.

Mindful evening activities are essential for unwinding and preparing for a restful night. Cooking dinner can become a mindful practice. Focus on chopping vegetables, the smell of spices, and the sizzle of food in the pan. When you sit down to eat, savor each bite, paying attention to the flavors, textures, and smells. This practice enhances your dining experience and helps you stay present and enjoy the moment. Engaging in a hobby with mindful awareness can also be incredibly relaxing. Whether knitting, painting, or playing a musical instrument, focus fully on the activity. Notice the feel of the yarn, the paint's colors, or the music's sound. This mindful engagement can provide a sense of calm and fulfillment.

Gentle evening yoga or stretching routines are another excellent way to unwind. Spend a few minutes stretching your body, focusing on how each movement feels. Poses like a child's pose, legs up the wall, and gentle twists can help release tension and prepare your body for sleep. Practicing these movements with mindful awareness enhances their relaxing effects, helping you release the day's stress.

Preparing for a restful night's sleep involves incorporating mindfulness practices that promote deep relaxation. Evening meditation or a body scan can be particularly effective. Find a comfortable position, close your eyes, and focus on your breath. Gradually scan your body from head to toe, noticing any areas of tension and consciously relaxing them. Guided visualization exercises for sleep can also be helpful. Imagine a peaceful scene, like a beach or forest, and immerse yourself in the details. This mental escape can help quiet your mind and prepare you for sleep. Techniques for releasing the day's stress before bed include writing down any lingering thoughts or worries in a journal. This practice can help clear your mind, making it easier to drift off to sleep.

Creating a calming sleep environment is crucial for promoting mindfulness and relaxation. Start by setting up a calming bedroom ambiance with soft lighting and soothing scents. Use dim lamps or candles to create a gentle, relaxing atmosphere. Essential oils like lavender or chamomile can be diffused to promote relaxation. Using weighted blankets or other comfort items can also enhance your sleep environment. Weighted blankets provide a sense of security and can help reduce anxiety. Removing electronics and creating a screen-free zone is another important step. The blue light from screens can interfere with your body's natural sleep-wake cycle. Instead, enjoy calming activities like reading a book, listening to soothing music, or practicing gentle stretches before bed. Screen-free time helps signal your body that it's time to wind down and prepare for sleep.

Weekly Mindfulness Check-In

Reflecting on the week is a powerful way to stay grounded and mindful. Each weekend, sit quietly with your journal and reflect on the past seven days. Start by considering what went well. Did you manage to stay present during a particularly stressful meeting? You may find a few moments of peace during your morning commute. Write these successes down. They are worth celebrating. Next, think about the areas where you struggled. Perhaps you needed help maintaining focus during the afternoon slump or felt overwhelmed by your to-do list. Acknowledge these challenges without judgment. Use journaling prompts to guide your reflection, such as "What moments this week brought me joy?" or "When did I feel most stressed?" This practice helps you gain insight into your mindfulness journey, showing you where you're thriving and where you might need a little more attention.

Setting mindful intentions for the upcoming week can give you a clear and purposeful direction. Start by thinking about what you want to achieve mentally and emotionally. Your intentions should be realistic and meaningful, focusing on how you want to feel rather than specific outcomes. For example, instead of completing a project by mid-week, aim to approach your work calmly and focus. Techniques for creating these intentions include visualizing a successful week ahead. Picture yourself navigating your days with ease and grace, handling challenges calmly. Reinforce these intentions with affirmations. Write statements like, "I am capable of managing my time effectively," or "I will approach each task with mindfulness and patience." These affirmations help solidify your intentions, making them a guiding force throughout the week.

Incorporating mindfulness into your weekly planning and scheduling can help you create a balanced and fulfilling routine. Start by reviewing your commitments and identifying where you can integrate mindfulness practices. Techniques for mindful time management include setting aside specific times for mindfulness breaks, such as a short meditation before lunch or a mindful walk in the afternoon. Create a balanced schedule that includes both work and self-care activities. For instance, if you have a busy Tuesday day, plan a relaxing evening activity like a warm bath or gentle yoga session to unwind. Planning mindful activities and self-care can help you maintain balance and prevent burnout. Make sure to include activities that bring you joy and relaxation, whether reading a book, gardening, or spending time with loved ones.

Self-care and rejuvenation are crucial aspects of the weekly check-in. Reflect on your self-care needs and consider how to meet them in the upcoming week. This might involve setting boundaries to protect your time and energy or scheduling activities that nourish your mind and body. Techniques for identifying self-care needs include listening to your body and noticing how you feel. Are you tired and need rest, or do you crave social connection? Plan self-care activities that align with these needs. Consider activities like a spa day at home, a nature walk, or a creative hobby for relaxation and rejuvenation. Practicing gratitude for the week's experiences can also enhance your well-being. Take a moment to reflect on the positive aspects of your week and express gratitude for them. This practice can shift your focus from what went wrong to what went right, fostering a more positive outlook.

Here's a reflection exercise to help you with your weekly mindfulness check-in:

Weekly Reflection Exercise

1. Celebrate Successes: Write down three moments from the past week where you felt mindful and present.
2. Identify Challenges: Note any situations where you struggled to maintain mindfulness. What contributed to these challenges?
3. Set Intentions: Write down one or two mindful intentions for the upcoming week. How do you want to feel? What mindset do you want to cultivate?
4. Plan Self-Care: List three self-care activities you will prioritize in the coming week. How will these activities support your well-being?

Ending each week with this mindful check-in can provide valuable insights, helping you grow and improve your mindfulness practice. You can create a more balanced and fulfilling life by reflecting on your experiences, setting meaningful intentions, planning mindfully, and prioritizing self-care. This practice enhances your mindfulness journey and supports your overall well-being, helping you navigate life's challenges with greater ease and grace.

TWELVE

Holistic Well-Being and Inclusivity

I remember a time when everything felt disconnected. My mind was always racing, my emotions were everywhere, and my body often felt like it was carrying the world's weight. It wasn't until I started exploring the mind-body connection that I understood how intertwined our mental, emotional, and physical health are. This realization was a game-changer. It showed me a path to a more balanced and fulfilling life.

Understanding the Mind-Body Connection

The concept of the mind-body connection is not new, but it often feels like a profound revelation when you experience it personally. The mind-body connection refers to the relationship between our thoughts, emotions, and physical health. Our mental state can significantly influence our physical state and vice versa. Historically, figures like Galen and Moses Maimonides recognized this link, and modern science has only bolstered these ancient insights.

Scientific research supports the idea that our thoughts and emotions can have a direct impact on our physical health. Studies have shown that stress, for instance, affects the autonomic nervous system and neuroendocrine function, leading to various health issues, including heart disease and diabetes (SOURCE 1). When we experience psychological stress, our body releases stress hormones like cortisol, which can cause inflammation and weaken the immune system. Over time, chronic stress can lead to damaging changes in organ systems, contributing to conditions such as hypertension, digestive problems, and even depression.

Understanding how deeply our thoughts and emotions impact our physical well-being is crucial. When you're anxious or stressed, your body responds by tightening muscles, increasing heart rate, and triggering a cascade of stress hormones. Conversely, when you practice mindfulness and positive thinking, your body can relax, reduce stress hormone levels, and promote healing. This intricate dance between mind and body underscores the importance of holistic well-being.

Benefits of a Strong Mind-Body Connection

Cultivating a strong mind-body connection offers numerous benefits. First and foremost, it can significantly improve your mental health and emotional regulation. When you're attuned to your body's signals, you can better manage anxiety, stress, and emotional fluctuations. This heightened awareness helps you respond to challenges with a calm and balanced mindset rather than reacting impulsively.

Another notable benefit is enhanced physical health. A strong mind-body connection can reduce chronic pain and improve overall physical well-being. For instance, mindful practices like meditation and yoga have been shown to lower blood pressure, improve heart health, and boost immune function. By paying attention to your body's needs and responding with care and compassion, you can alleviate physical discomfort and promote healing.

Overall well-being and life satisfaction also improve when you nurture this connection. When you feel physically healthy and emotionally balanced, you're more likely to experience a sense of fulfillment and joy in your daily life. This holistic approach to well-being fosters a deeper appreciation for the present moment and a greater sense of inner peace.

Mindfulness Techniques to Strengthen the Connection

Several mindfulness techniques can help you strengthen the mind-body connection. One effective practice is body scan meditation, which involves paying close attention to different parts of your body, from your toes to the top of your head. This practice helps you become aware of physical sensations, areas of tension, and overall body awareness. By regularly tuning into your body, you can better understand its needs and respond with care.

Mindful breathing is another powerful technique. By focusing on your breath, you can synchronize your mind and body, creating a sense of harmony and balance. Deep, intentional breathing helps calm the nervous system, reduce stress, and improve mental clarity. Practicing mindful breathing throughout the day, especially during stressful moments, can help you stay grounded and centered.

Visualization exercises also enhance the mind-body connection. These exercises involve imagining peaceful and healing scenes, such as a serene beach or a lush forest. By visualizing these calming environments, you can evoke a sense of relaxation and well-being in your body. Visualization can also mentally rehearse positive outcomes, boosting confidence and reducing anxiety.

Real-Life Applications

The benefits of a strong mind-body connection extend to various aspects of life. For instance, athletes often use mindful movement techniques to improve their performance. Focusing on their breath and bodily sensations can enhance their coordination, stamina, and overall physical capabilities. This mindful approach helps them stay present and perform at their best.

Other significant benefits include enhanced creativity and problem-solving ability. When your mind and body are in sync, you can tap into a deeper well of creativity and innovation. Mindfulness practices help clear mental clutter, allowing you to think more clearly and approach problems with fresh perspectives. This heightened creativity can benefit both personal and professional endeavors.

Better stress management and resilience are the most impactful benefits of a strong mind-body connection. In the face of life's challenges, being attuned to your body and emotions helps you navigate stress with grace and poise. Mindfulness practices equip you with the tools to remain calm, centered, and resilient, even in the most trying times. This resilience improves your well-being and enhances your ability to support and connect with others.

Reflection Exercise: Exploring Your Mind-Body Connection

Take a few moments to reflect on your current mind-body connection. Sit in a quiet space, close your eyes, and take a few deep breaths. Pay attention to any sensations in your body—tension, warmth, coolness. Notice how your thoughts and emotions might be influencing these sensations. Write down your observations and consider incorporating mindfulness practices to strengthen this connection. This exercise can help you develop a deeper awareness of your mind-body relationship and guide you toward holistic well-being.

Mindful Stretching Exercises

Mindful stretching is more than just a series of physical movements. It's an intentional practice that blends the benefits of stretching with mindfulness to create a holistic mind and body experience. This practice involves paying close attention to the sensations in your body as you stretch, noticing how each movement feels, and staying present in the moment. Unlike traditional stretching, which often focuses solely on physical flexibility or exercise preparation, mindful stretching cultivates mental relaxation and emotional balance. It's about connecting with your body, easing tension, and finding calm.

The benefits of mindful stretching are numerous. Physically, it enhances flexibility and reduces muscle tension, alleviating pain and improving overall mobility. Mentally, it promotes relaxation, reduces stress, and enhances your awareness of how your body feels. Integrating mindfulness into your stretching routine can also improve your emotional well-being, as this practice encourages you to be kind and patient with yourself. It's a gentle way to nurture your body and mind, fostering a deeper connection.

Let's start with some basic mindful stretching exercises. One of my favorites is the gentle neck and shoulder stretch. Begin by sitting comfortably with your back straight. Slowly tilt your head to one side, bringing your ear towards your shoulder. Hold the stretch for a few breaths, feeling the gentle pull along the side of your neck. Repeat on the other side. Next, try the seated forward bend. Sit with your legs extended straight in front of you. Inhale deeply, then exhale as you gently reach for your toes, allowing your spine to lengthen. This stretch can help relieve lower back tension. Another simple yet effective stretch is the standing side stretch. Stand with your feet hip-width apart, raise your arms overhead, and clasp your hands together. Gently lean to one side, feeling the stretch along your side body. Hold for a few breaths, then switch sides.

Incorporating these stretches into your daily routine can make a significant difference in how you feel. Start your day with a morning stretching routine to awaken your body and mind. Spend a few minutes stretching as soon as you get out of bed, focusing on how each movement feels. Midday stretches can be a great way to relieve work-related tension. If you spend long hours at a desk, take short breaks to stretch your neck, shoulders, and back. These moments of mindfulness can refresh your mind and reduce stress. Consider a gentle stretching session in the evening to unwind and prepare for a restful sleep. Combining stretches with deep breathing can help you release the day's tension and promote relaxation.

Advanced mindful stretching exercises offer additional benefits for those looking to deepen their practice. Yoga-inspired stretches like the cat-cow or child's pose can provide deeper relaxation and flexibility. In the cat-cow pose, you move between arching and rounding your spine while synchronizing your breath with each movement. This dynamic stretch enhances spinal flexibility and promotes mindfulness through breath awareness. Dynamic stretching combined with mindful breathing can further enhance the mind-body connection. For example, flowing through gentle movements while focusing on your breath can create a meditative state, reducing stress and increasing mindfulness.

Partner stretching can also be a wonderful way to enhance connection and support. When you stretch with a partner, you rely on each other for balance and stability, fostering trust and communication. This practice can especially benefit couples or friends looking to deepen their bond through shared mindfulness. One simple partner stretch is the seated forward bend with a partner. Sit facing each other with your legs extended and feet touching. Hold each other's hands and take turns gently pulling each other forward into a stretch. Communication is key; ensure you're comfortable and supportive throughout the movement.

Mindful stretching is a versatile practice that can fit seamlessly into your daily life. Whether you're looking to relieve physical tension, reduce stress, or simply take a few moments for yourself, these exercises offer a holistic approach to well-being. By paying attention to your body and staying present in the moment, you can cultivate a sense of inner peace and connection that extends beyond the physical benefits of stretching. So, take a deep breath, stretch mindfully, and embrace this practice's calm and clarity.

Inclusivity in Mindfulness Practices

Inclusivity in mindfulness practices is about creating a space where everyone feels welcome, respected, and valued. It means acknowledging and honoring the diverse backgrounds, experiences, and perspectives that individuals bring to their mindfulness journey. By fostering an inclusive environment, we can enrich our mindfulness practice and build a supportive community that benefits everyone. Inclusivity allows us to learn from each other, share our unique insights, and grow together. It's about creating a space where everyone feels seen and heard, regardless of background or beliefs.

Diverse perspectives in mindfulness practice offer a wealth of benefits. We can draw on a broader range of wisdom and techniques when we include different spiritual and cultural traditions. This diversity can deepen our understanding and enhance our practice. For example, incorporating elements from Buddhist, Hindu, Christian, Indigenous, and other spiritual traditions can provide new insights and approaches to mindfulness. Using inclusive language in mindfulness instruction is also crucial. It ensures that everyone feels welcome and respected, regardless of their background. This might mean avoiding jargon or specific religious terminology and instead using language that is accessible and inviting to all.

Creating an inclusive mindfulness space involves thoughtful attention to the physical and emotional environment. Start by creating a space that reflects diverse cultural elements, such as artwork, symbols, or objects from different traditions. This can create a sense of belonging and respect for all participants. Ensuring accessibility for individuals with disabilities is also vital. This might include providing seating options, ensuring physical access, and offering materials in different formats, such as Braille or large print. Promoting belonging through mindful community activities can help everyone feel included. Organize events or practices that invite people to share their unique perspectives and experiences. This could be as simple as a sharing circle where everyone has the opportunity to speak or more structured activities like workshops or cultural celebrations.

Mindfulness can also be a powerful tool for promoting social justice and inclusivity. By practicing mindfulness in activism, we can approach social justice work with compassion, clarity, and resilience. Techniques such as mindful listening and holding space for others can foster empathy and understanding. Guided meditations focused on empathy and compassion can help us connect with others' experiences and motivations, deepening our commitment to social justice. Personal stories of using mindfulness for social change illustrate its potential. For example, one activist found that mindfulness helped her stay grounded and focused during protests, allowing her to respond to challenges calmly and clearly. Another used mindfulness to navigate difficult conversations about race and privilege, fostering deeper understanding and connection.

Ultimately, inclusivity in mindfulness practices creates a space where everyone can thrive. It's about embracing diversity, honoring different perspectives, and building a supportive, compassionate community. Whether practicing alone or with others, strive to create an inclusive environment that welcomes and respects everyone. This enriches your practice and builds a stronger, more connected community. By incorporating diverse perspectives, using inclusive language, creating accessible spaces, and promoting social justice, we can make mindfulness a truly inclusive practice. This approach benefits individuals and strengthens the community, fostering connections and promoting well-being for all.

Building a Supportive Community

The role of the community in maintaining holistic well-being cannot be overstated. Social support is a crucial factor in mental and physical health. Having a network of people who understand and support you can significantly reduce feelings of stress and loneliness. Studies have shown that strong social connections can improve immune function, lower rates of anxiety and depression, and even increase longevity. Mindfulness naturally fosters these connections by encouraging empathy and understanding. Mindfulness can strengthen bonds, enhance emotional resilience, and create a shared sense of purpose when practiced within a community.

Creating a mindful community starts with organizing groups and meetups where people can practice mindfulness. This could be as simple as a weekly meditation session at a local park or a more structured group that meets regularly to discuss mindfulness topics and share experiences. Facilitating mindful group activities is essential for nurturing these communities. Begin with a group check-in where everyone can share their current state of mind. Follow it with a guided meditation or a mindfulness exercise, such as mindful walking or eating. Ensure each session ends with a reflection period where participants can discuss their experiences and insights.

Setting guidelines for a supportive and inclusive community is crucial. Establish norms that promote respect, empathy, and non-judgment. Encourage open communication and create a safe space where everyone feels heard and valued. These guidelines help maintain a positive and nurturing environment, allowing the community to thrive. When everyone understands and respects the group's principles, it creates a foundation of trust and mutual support. This foundation is vital for the community's resilience, especially during challenging times.

Mindful communication within the community is another essential aspect. Practicing active listening in group settings can significantly strengthen connections. Encourage participants to listen fully without interrupting, reflecting on what they've heard to ensure understanding. This practice fosters deeper empathy and reduces misunderstandings. Techniques for expressing emotions mindfully can also enhance communication. Encourage members to use "I" statements to share their feelings and needs, which can help prevent conflicts and promote open dialogue. When conflicts arise, mindful dialogue can be an effective tool for resolution. This involves staying present, focusing on the issue at hand, and approaching the conversation with an open and non-judgmental mindset.

Sustaining community engagement over time requires regular check-ins and reflections. Schedule periodic reviews to assess the group's progress and address any challenges. These check-ins can help keep everyone aligned with the community's goals and ensure the group remains supportive and inclusive. Planning mindful events and retreats can also sustain engagement. Organize activities like weekend retreats, workshops, or mindfulness-themed social events to deepen connections and provide growth opportunities. These events can offer a break from daily routines and create memorable shared experiences that strengthen the community bond.

Another effective strategy is creating online platforms for ongoing support and connection. Use social media groups, forums, or messaging apps to maintain communication between meetups. These platforms can be spaces for sharing resources, offering support, and continuing discussions. They also allow members who cannot attend in-person meetings to stay connected. Regularly updating these platforms with new content and encouraging active participation can keep the community engaged and vibrant.

Building a supportive community through mindfulness practices enhances well-being on multiple levels. It fosters social connections, empathy, and resilience, providing a strong foundation for individual and collective growth. You can create a vibrant community that nurtures everyone involved by organizing mindful groups, facilitating activities, setting supportive guidelines, practicing mindful communication, and sustaining engagement. This holistic approach benefits each member and strengthens the community as a whole, promoting a sense of belonging and shared purpose.

Conclusion

As we end our journey together, I want to remind you of the vision that inspired this book: empowering you to cultivate emotional balance, inner calm, and self-acceptance through mindfulness. It's been a heartfelt mission to provide you with tools and techniques to help lighten the heavy loads of perfectionism, anxiety, and control. I hope that you feel more equipped to embrace peace in your daily life.

Throughout the chapters, we've explored various aspects of mindfulness and how it can transform your relationship with yourself and the world around you. We started with the power of self-compassion, learning how to treat ourselves with the same kindness we offer others. We delved into the basics of mindfulness, understanding its principles and the science behind it.

We discussed practical techniques like mindful breathing, body scan, and walking meditation, which are simple yet powerful practices that ground you in the present moment. We addressed specific challenges like managing anxiety, overcoming negative self-talk, and balancing multiple roles, each with tailored mindfulness exercises to make these tasks more manageable.

One of the key takeaways is that mindfulness is more than achieving perfection or always being calm. It's about being present and aware, accepting whatever arises with an open heart. It's about recognizing that it's okay to have flaws and that these imperfections make us human. It's about finding moments of peace amidst the chaos and learning to be gentle with ourselves in times of struggle.

Another important point is the interconnectedness of our mental, emotional, and physical well-being. Practicing mindfulness can strengthen this mind-body connection, leading to improved health and a deeper sense of fulfillment. Techniques like mindful stretching and body scan meditation can help you become more attuned to your body's signals, promoting overall wellness.

As you continue on this path, remember that mindfulness is a journey, not a destination. It's not about doing it perfectly but about showing up consistently. The practices and exercises we've covered are tools for your toolbox. Use them regularly, and they will become second nature. Integrate them into your daily routine through mindful mornings, mindful work breaks, or evening wind-downs.

I encourage you to take specific actions to maintain your mindfulness practice. Set aside a few minutes each day for meditation or mindful breathing. Create a dedicated space in your home to retreat for a moment of calm. Join a mindfulness group or community to share your experiences and gain support. Reflect on your progress through journaling and celebrate your small victories along the way.

I am deeply grateful to you for embarking on this journey with me and for allowing this book to be part of your path toward inner peace. Your willingness to explore these practices and make them a part of your life is truly inspiring.

Remember, you are not alone in this journey. We all face challenges and have moments of doubt and struggle. But we can find strength, resilience, and a sense of peace through mindfulness. Embrace your imperfections because they are what make you unique. Find joy in the present moment, even in the simplest of things. Continue cultivating emotional resilience and inner peace, knowing that every step you take is toward a more balanced and fulfilling life.

Keep going, keep practicing, and keep believing in yourself. You have everything you need within you to create a life of emotional balance and inner calm. And whenever you need a reminder or a bit of encouragement, this book will always be here for you.

With heartfelt gratitude and warmest wishes,

EveMeadows

References

- *Self-Compassion Research by Kristin Neff* https://self-compassion.org/the-research/
- *The Role of Self-Compassion in Development: A Healthier ...* https://www.ncbi.nlm.nih.gov/pmc/articles/PMC2790748/
- *The Five Myths of Self-Compassion* https://greatergood.berkeley.edu/article/item/the_five_myths_of_self_compassion
- *10 Ways to Overcome Perfectionism – Oregon Counseling* https://oregoncounseling.com/article/10-ways-to-overcome-perfectionism/
- *When science meets mindfulness - Harvard Gazette* https://news.harvard.edu/gazette/story/2018/04/harvard-researchers-study-how-mindfulness-may-change-the-brain-in-depressed-patients/
- *Neural mechanisms of mindfulness and meditation* https://www.ncbi.nlm.nih.gov/pmc/articles/PMC4109098/
- *Mindfulness and Emotion Regulation: Insights from ...* https://www.ncbi.nlm.nih.gov/pmc/articles/PMC5337506/
- *Communicating Mindfully in Relationships* https://www.psychologytoday.com/us/blog/conscious-communication/201709/communicating-mindfully-in-relationships
- *Mindful Breathing: Benefits, Types, and Scripts* https://psychcentral.com/health/mindful-breathing
- *Body Scan Meditation: Benefits and How to Do It* https://www.verywellmind.com/body-scan-meditation-why-and-how-3144782
- *Walking Meditation* https://www.headspace.com/meditation/walking-meditation
- *Mindful Eating: The Art of Presence While You Eat - PMC* https://www.ncbi.nlm.nih.gov/pmc/articles/PMC5556586/
- *How to Use Mindfulness Therapy for Anxiety: 15 Exercises* https://positivepsychology.com/mindfulness-for-anxiety/
- *8 Breathing Exercises for Anxiety You Can Try Right Now* https://www.healthline.com/health/breathing-exercises-for-anxiety
- *30 Grounding Techniques to Quiet Distressing Thoughts* https://www.healthline.com/health/grounding-techniques
- *From Chaos to Calm: How to Create a Zen Space at Home ...* https://marblewellness.com/post/from-chaos-to-calm-how-to-create-a-zen-space-at-home-for-anxiety-relief/

- *How to Identify and Manage Your Emotional Triggers* https://www.healthline.com/health/mental-health/emotional-triggers
- *Mindfulness and Emotion Regulation: Insights from …* https://www.ncbi.nlm.nih.gov/pmc/articles/PMC5337506/
- *Cognitive-Behavioral Treatments for Anxiety and Stress- …* https://www.ncbi.nlm.nih.gov/pmc/articles/PMC8475916/
- *The Relationship Between Mindfulness and Resilience* https://psychcentral.com/lib/mindfulness-the-art-of-cultivating-resilience
- *The Toxic Effects of Negative Self-Talk* https://www.verywellmind.com/negative-self-talk-and-how-it-affects-us-4161304
- *Cognitive Restructuring: Techniques and Examples* https://www.healthline.com/health/cognitive-restructuring
- *Exercise 2: Self-Compassion Break* https://self-compassion.org/exercises/exercise-2-self-compassion-break/
- *Mental Health Journaling: The Benefits of Writing for …* https://dayoneapp.com/blog/mental-health-journaling/
- *Toward a realistic approach to Mindfulness and Time …* https://connect.mayoclinic.org/blog/mindfulness-in-health/newsfeed-post/toward-a-realistic-approach-to-mindfulness-and-time-management/
- *Compassionate Boundaries: How to Say No with Heart* https://www.mindful.org/compassionate-boundaries-say-no-heart/
- *Parenting-focused mindfulness intervention reduces stress …* https://www.ncbi.nlm.nih.gov/pmc/articles/PMC7962755/
- *Relieve Stress with These 8 Tips for Creating a Mindful …* https://www.psychedconsult.com/relieve-stress-with-these-8-tips-for-creating-a-mindful-space-in-the-home/
- *Here and now: Discover the benefits of being present* https://www.betterup.com/blog/how-to-be-present
- *How to Use Mindfulness Therapy for Anxiety: 15 Exercises* https://positivepsychology.com/mindfulness-for-anxiety/
- *How to Forgive Yourself With Self-Compassion* https://www.psychologytoday.com/us/blog/striving-thriving/202207/how-forgive-yourself-self-compassion
- *Tips, Practices, and Activities for Mindful Communication* https://www.mindfulteachers.org/blog/mindful-communication
- *Meditation: A simple, fast way to reduce stress* https://www.mayoclinic.org/tests-procedures/meditation/in-depth/meditation/art-20045858
- *The Transformative Effects of Mindful Self-Compassion* https://www.mindful.org/the-transformative-effects-of-mindful-self-compassion/

- *Brief Mindfulness Meditation Improves Emotion Processing* https://www.ncbi.nlm.nih.gov/pmc/articles/PMC6795685/
- *How to Use Meditation for Better Sleep* https://www.healthline.com/health/meditation-for-sleep
- *Present Tense: 7 Mindfulness Strategies to Cope with Loss* https://www.healthline.com/health/mind-body/mindfulness-strategies-to-cope-with-loss
- *Communicating Mindfully in Relationships* https://www.psychologytoday.com/us/blog/conscious-communication/201709/communicating-mindfully-in-relationships
- *Use mindfulness to cope with chronic pain* https://www.mayoclinichealthsystem.org/hometown-health/speaking-of-health/use-mindfulness-to-cope-with-chronic-pain
- *30 Grounding Techniques to Quiet Distressing Thoughts* https://www.healthline.com/health/grounding-techniques
- *How To Create A Mindful Morning Routine* https://www.thegoodtrade.com/features/creating-a-mindful-morning-routine/
- *Transform Your Daily Commute (10 Mindful Techniques for a ...* https://moveinsync.medium.com/10-techniques-for-mindful-commuting-a5cb8aae0f36
- *How to Manage Stress with Mindfulness and Meditation* https://www.mindful.org/how-to-manage-stress-with-mindfulness-and-meditation/
- *Evening Meditation: Your Path to Stress-Free Nights* https://blog.mindvalley.com/evening-meditation/
- *Mind–body research moves towards the mainstream - NCBI* https://www.ncbi.nlm.nih.gov/pmc/articles/PMC1456909/
- *MINDFUL STRETCHINGGUIDE* https://uhs.berkeley.edu/sites/default/files/wellness-mindfulstretchingguide.pdf
- *3 Mindfulness Practices for Neurodiverse Meditators* https://www.mindful.org/3-mindfulness-practices-for-neurodiverse-meditators/
- *Section 8. Mindfulness and Community Building* https://ctb.ku.edu/en/table-of-contents/spirituality-and-community-building/mindfulness-community-building/main

www.ingramcontent.com/pod-product-compliance
Lightning Source LLC
Chambersburg PA
CBHW060904140726
47996CB00001B/106